The USPI
Urban Self Defense
Manual

Balogun Ojetade

ISBN: 1537628194
ISBN-13: 978-1537628196

DEDICATION

To every Afrikan that fights – and fought – against the system of Global
White Supremacy.
Ever.

CONTENTS

ACKNOWLEDGMENTS

I would like to thank all of the organizations that work diligently to make life better for Afrikans worldwide, with special thanks to: the Urban Survival Preparedness Institute, the Afrikan Martial Arts Institute, the FTP Movement, the Coalition to Combat Police Terrorism, the Black Empowerment Council, Freedom Home Academy International, Akoben Institute, and the Davis Bozeman Law Firm.

INTRODUCTION

I have always been a prepper; all my life.

When I was 6 years old in third grade – yes, I was a bit advanced; PLUS my godmother was assistant principal at my school – we were asked to draw where we would like to live when we "grow up." All the children, except me, drew "exotic" locales, mostly in Paris – for some odd reason Black folks used to believe the French treat us better than other Caucasians and there is no racism in France. I suppose some STILL believe such foolishness; I never did.

When my teacher – a hippy Caucasian woman – got to my drawing, she paused and her smile faded. She put the drawing to the side and then returned to the pile of other drawings by my classmates. Her smile returned. I wondered why she put my drawing to the side, but shrugged it off and went back to whispering jokes with my friends.

When recess-time came, I lined up with the rest of the children to go outside and play for 15 minutes. The teacher told me to stay behind. I was visibly disappointed. She promised to let me go outside 10 minutes early during our second recess, so I complied.

The teacher held up my artwork and said "Explain this to me, please."

"That's my house," I said, pointing at a large, two-story house encircled by tall trees. "And that's my tunnel that leads to my armored off-road vehicle and THAT's my tunnel that leads to the river, where my boat is."

"And what's this?" she asked, pointing at my drawing of a brown man firing a rifle at pink men in blue uniforms and pink and brown men in green uniforms.

"That's me killing the police and the National Guard when they come for me just before the government declares a race war," I replied.

My teacher swallowed hard. "And why are they coming after YOU?"

"Because I have weapons, supplies and survival skills and worse, I teach my people those same skills," I said.

The teacher swallowed hard again. "Okay," she croaked. "But I need you to draw a nicer picture we can put up on the wall. This one might scare some children...and some parents if they see it."

"Okay," I said. "I'll draw you a lie."

And that was that. I drew her a picture of me with a wife and three children – I had no idea I would end up with *eight* – as we visited Disney World. She was satisfied. I took my first drawing home and my parents got a kick out of it. My father's only critique was that I should dispatch them silently – with a bow or blade – so I don't alert the full force of the enemy to my presence.

"Good teaching," I said, nodding in agreement.

My father laughed.

Fast forward to my senior year in high school – my A.P. Social Studies teacher gave us a project for our final: write a dissertation on some social issue and successfully defend it. I chose genocide of people of Afrikan descent in the U.S. This was long before the time of the internet and my set of encyclopedias offered little in the way of information on the topic. The public libraries did not offer much more. I decided to try the D'Angelo Law Library at the University of Chicago. The lead librarian told me that only students of the University of Chicago Law School and U of C pre-law students in at least their junior year could enter the library and use its resources.

I lied and said I was a pre-law senior, but left my student identification back at my apartment. The librarian laughed. She gave me a temporary card and said I could use the facility until the library closed, but that would be the end of it. I thanked her and went to work. As I figured, the library had quite a bit on genocide. I gathered up several books and furiously scribbled notes.

At the end of the night, the librarian asked if I got all I needed. "No," I replied. "But thank you, so much, for your help."

"You give up too easily," she said. "See you tomorrow."

I thanked her again and left. I returned the next day and the next day and the next. By that Thursday, I had all I needed. As I was leaving, the librarian showed me a photo of her mother – a dark skinned Black woman. I was shocked; I thought she was an elderly Caucasian lady.

"Do us proud with that project," she said. "My sister was sterilized while she was in jail, which is why I and the rest of my siblings decided to pass. Be careful, though."

"Yes, ma'am," I said as I darted out the door. I didn't know what she meant by be careful, but I felt the weight of her words.

My dissertation sparked a minor civil war at my school. Caucasian students in my class tried to dismiss genocide on Africans in America as a myth. One even said "You're co-opting what happened to Jews and trying to say it's happening to Blacks!" That got a lot of students up in arms and the divide between Black students and Caucasian ones was an obvious one.

I received the highest score in the class due to

the dissertation and my defense of it, though.

Three days later, after things calmed down at the school, my Social Studies teacher had me stay behind after class.

"Are you in the Nation of Islam?" she asked.

"No," I answered.

"You WILL be," she said. "Just know that from this day forward, you are being watched."

"By who?" I inquired.

"You KNOW who," she whispered. "Be careful!"

I nodded and left the class.

She was right...on ALL accounts. A few years later, I did, indeed, become a Registered Muslim at Mosque Number 2 ("Mosque Maryam") in Chicago and remained in the Nation of Islam for 12 years. AND I now know who watches me and why. But I am ready for the watchers when they stop watching and make their move.

As I said, I have always been a prepper; all my life.

If you aren't, you'd better become one...NOW!

Origins of Urban Survival and Self-Defense

Since the creation of Afrikan civilization, man has created an artificial environment in which to live – towns; villages; cities; kingdoms; empires. Part of the function of this urban environment is to separate us from the rest of nature and protect us from natural disasters, climate, predators and our enemies.

We may have escaped being eaten by a leopard, but the leopard has been replaced by other predators – the police; and, in some instances, the military. And packs of wolves, hyenas, and coyotes have been replaced by the system of global white supremacy and its agents. Even though we have some protection from the natural disasters of droughts and floods, we are still subject to the man-made disasters of police terrorism and governmental tyranny.

Our ancient ancestors survived all dangers and disasters because they possessed the ultimate weapon: their intellect. Ancient man learned the behavior patterns of predators, and the laws of nature. These patterns have changed little.

By learning to observe and recognize the behaviors of predators, and the signs of impending turmoil, the modern Afrikan warrior can likewise survive the challenges and dangers of the urban environment.

How to Use this Manual

Like any technical manual, this book contains more information than can be digested in a single reading, so study it in sections, then put into practice what you read. Once you are comfortable executing the skills in that section, move on to another section and so on. In this way you won't feel overwhelmed and the lessons will truly sink in.

CHAPTER ONE
SURVIVING PREDATORS

In the urban environment, criminals fulfill nature's role of predators. When we say criminals in this book, this includes the police – serial killing, mass murder, assault and battery are crimes, after all, and no one has perpetrated these crimes upon Afrikans worldwide longer than, and more frequently than, the police.

"Impossible!" you cry. "Officer Friendly gave me a coloring book and crayons when I was five."

And when you were fifteen, YOU became the coloring book and that same "Officer Friendly" painted the pavement RED with your blood after he busted your head to the WHITE meat and left you seeing YELLOW stars and GREEN clovers through two BLACK eyes.

The continued enslavement and control of Afrikans are the motivations shaping early policing. Those motivations have not changed.

Slave patrols and Night Watches, which later became modern police departments, were both designed to control the behaviors of Afrikans. In 1704, the colony of Carolina developed the nation's first slave patrol. Slave patrols helped to maintain the economic order and to assist the wealthy landowners in recovering and punishing enslaved Afrikans who essentially were considered property.

Policing was not the only social institution enmeshed in slavery. Slavery was fully institutionalized in the American economic and legal order with laws being enacted at both the state and national divisions of government. Virginia, for example, enacted more than 130 slave statutes between 1689 and 1865. Slavery and the abuse of people of Afrikan descent, however, was not merely a "southern thang," as many have been miseducated to believe. Connecticut, New York and other colonies enacted laws to criminalize and control enslaved Afrikans. In 1793 and 1850, Congress passed fugitive *Slave Laws*, laws allowing the detention and return of Afrikans who escaped kidnapping.

The legacy of slavery and racism did not end after the Civil War, of course. In fact it can be argued that extreme violence against Afrikans became even worse with the rise of vigilante groups who resisted Reconstruction. These vigilantes were lynch mobs that became notorious for hanging Afrikans. Perhaps the most infamous American vigilante group, the Ku Klux Klan, started in the 1860s, was notorious for assaulting and lynching Black men for transgressions that would not be considered crimes at all had a White man committed them. Lynching occurred across the entire country, not just in the South. Finally, in 1871

Congress passed the Ku Klux Klan Act, which prohibited state actors from violating the Civil Rights of all citizens in part **because of law enforcements' involvement with the infamous group**.

I stumbled upon a classic American folk song a years ago. It's called *Run, Nigger, Run.*

This tune – under the variant title *Run, Boy, Run* – is an old-time country music standard.

This song was recorded in 1927 by the band the *Skillet Lickers.* These are the lyrics they sang:

Run nigger run, the pateroller catch you,

Run nigger run, well you better get away…

Nigger run, nigger flew,

Nigger tore his shirt in two,

Run, run, the pateroller catch you,

Run nigger run, well you better get away.

Just so you know, the *Skillet Lickers* were a popular and influential group that recorded this song – and more than 100 others – for Columbia Records.

Also, they did not write it. *Run, Nigger, Run* was already a part of Southern folklore and was originally a *Black* folk song. More precisely, a song sung by enslaved Afrikans.

The song was referred to by elderly ex-slaves in various documented "slave narratives."

Harre Quarls of Texas remembered: "Us couldn't go anywhere 'cept us have pass from our massa to 'nother. If us slips off, dem patterrollers gits us. Patterroller hits 39 licks with de rawhide with de nine tails. Patterroller gits 50 cents for hittin' us 39 licks.

"Captain, here am de words to de patterroller song: 'Run, nigger, run, patterroller cotch you...' "

Likewise, Cresa Mack of Arkansas told an interviewer: "I remember that they used to sing: 'Run nigger run, the paddy rollers catch you...' Course if they catch you without pass, they'd beat you nearly to death, and tell you to go home to your master."

The most detailed recollection comes from a man named Sylvia Floyd of Mississippi. Here is what Mr. Floyd told a U.S. government interviewer, exactly as it was rendered in the official transcript:

Sylvia Floyd: "...Dey never let 'em leave de plantation wid out a pass, an' dey had patrole riders to go out an' git 'em ifen dey didn't come in. Dey didn't hab to be much late 'fore yo' could hear 'em commin' after 'em.

De darkies use to pull pranks on de patrole riders by strechin' grape vines across de road to throw de horses. At other times de slaves 'ud git a little riled up an' jump de traces a little by fightin' back wid fire, but dey couldn't never do much fer dey never was allowed to git together enough to carry out nothin'. De patrole riders kept 'em purty well rounded up an' seperated only 'cept long enuf fer a little frolicin'.

Dey use to sing dis ole song 'bout 'em:

Run, nigger, run, de patrole's a commin',

Run, nigger, run, de patrole's a commin',

Dat nigger run, dat nigger flew

Dat nigger tore his shirt in two

Run, nigger, run!"

Types of Criminals

While the strategies criminals use vary widely, there is an important distinction between two types of criminal: the psychopathic, and the non-psychopathic.

The *non-psychopathic* criminal is the type most familiar to the public. For these criminals, crime is a survival mechanism anthropologists call the Cheating Strategy. The Cheating Strategy simply refers to the advantage cheating provides in terms of survival. For example, a person may spend eight hours a day working to earn a certain amount of money, but a thief could spend only a few minutes to gain what another spent eight hours to acquire. The thief's cheating strategy is cost effective – the gains far exceed expenditures.

However, we Afrikans are social animals and cheaters are seldom tolerated in a society wherein everyone works together for common benefits and equal share in the fruits thereof. Afrikan society evolved the institution of revenge and punishment as a counter to the cheating strategy. A thief who steals another's wages may be acting cost effectively, but if the thief is subsequently caught and his dominant hand is cut off, he will find the costs now far exceed the benefits.

Therefore, crime prevention requires that we make the costs of using a cheating strategy greater than the benefits by forcing criminals to work harder, and increasing their chances of being caught and when they are caught, they must be swiftly and harshly punished.

The cheating strategy is often used when people are at a disadvantage. This type of crime is logical. One person has something another does not, and so the latter cheats to acquire it. While we should not condone the methods employed, we can understand the motivation for the actions.

Another type of criminal behavior committed by non-psychopaths are crimes of passion. These acts of violence stem from emotional turmoil and our primitive instincts. Many otherwise average people are capable of committing assault, rape, and murder in the heat of passion especially if fueled by drugs and alcohol. While the acts they commit are pathological, they are not themselves necessarily psychopaths.

However, when it comes to the second type of criminal the underlying motivations become surreal. While psychopaths will certainly use the cheating strategy, it is seldom necessary to their survival. A millionaire psychopath would readily rob a starving child. Obviously, the millionaire's survival is not at stake. There is no obvious logic to what motives could underlie such behavior. Psychopaths often elude justice for this very reason. In criminal trials, the prosecution is required to ascribe a motive to the defendant. However, in the case of psychopaths, their motives are so bizarre and alien that even if a prosecutor could explain it, most jurors would not believe it. The psychopath can also assault, rape, and murder, but it is seldom a crime of passion. It is instead a cold and calculated plan to gain what the psychopath wants.

Most police officers who brutalize, rape and murder are psychopathic criminals. There are, however, many who commit such crimes for money or an advancement in position.

Of all the criminal types that inhabit our society, the psychopath is by far the most destructive, the most successful, and the least understood. For these reasons, any self-defense program must begin with a study of the most dangerous predator on the planet.

The Psychopath

Most people think of a psychopath as a monster in human flesh: Hannibal Lecter; Dexter; Michael Myers, from the movie *Halloween.*

Of course, the media tries to portray Black neighborhoods as the real-life breeding ground of the insane. However, you are more likely to find psychopaths in the boardroom than in the 'hood.

Why?

Because the more competitive a particular environment is, the more ruthless the use of the Cheating Strategy becomes.

Within the highest circles of power and wealth, a lack of pity and remorse is practically a prerequisite to success, and only the psychopathic mentality can thrive.

Because of the tremendous destruction psychopaths reap on society, it is vital for everyone to be aware of their existence and to recognize their behavior traits. Understanding them is the first step to defending yourself against them.

Key Characteristics of Psychopaths

- *Lack of Empathy:* Empathy is the ability to experience, within oneself, the feelings and emotions expressed by others. It is what allows us to feel what others are feeling. It is why we are inspired by works of art, music and poetry. Empathy allows us to experience the grandeur of life, to be truly alive, and is one of the defining characteristics of what makes us human. Psychopaths have no empathy and as a result, they are neither truly human, nor truly alive. When they see 'normal folks' admiring a piece of art, or playing with their children, or caring for a pet, or any number of human emotional interactions, they cannot understand what all the fuss is about. Psychopaths realize at an early age that they are different, and that they should act as everyone else does in order to be accepted into society. They learn to mimic what they see others do, but they can never understand why they should act this way.

Although they are consummate actors, careful observation will reveal telltale cracks in their façade. They know enough to fake concern when someone is sick, or to pretend happiness when some good fortune befalls a friend, but in situations where the psychopath has no pre-rehearsed act; their adlib often reveals a stunning lack of empathy. For example, if attending a comedy show, a psychopath would correctly mimic the same expressions of glee as the other members of the audience, but if a comedian was to suddenly grip his chest, scream in pain and then pass out on stage, he would still laugh, clueless to the gross inappropriateness of such an action. People with empathy would instinctively understand such behavior as inappropriate. The psychopath, however, cannot.

- *Lack of Remorse:* Remorse is an emotional expression of personal regret felt by a person after he or she has committed an act that they deem to be shameful, hurtful, or violent. This very definition precludes a psychopath from experiencing such a feeling. With no empathy, there can be no emotional expression. Nor can a psychopath feel shame, or comprehend that anything they do can be hurtful to others.

Psychopaths understand when people are angry with them for their behavior, and as a last resort, they may pretend they are sorry, but unlike most people, they are not the least bit disturbed by feelings of guilt. Remorse is a powerful negative emotion that causes turmoil in those that feel it, turmoil that often results in self-destructive or self-deprecating behaviors. The psychopath may pretend remorse but their real behavior has not changed, they still go shopping, they still go to parties, they have no problems sleeping at night.

- *Superficiality:* Passion drives someone to go further than needed to explore, learn, and master a subject. Most people enjoy listening to music, but it is someone passionate about music that goes on to learn how to play an instrument. Similarly, many people are interested in new technology but only a passionate person goes on to become an engineer. Lacking passion for anything other than themselves, psychopaths can never penetrate beyond the surface of most knowledge. As a result, they exhibit a "superficial" comprehension of some or many subjects but are often seen by true experts as being shallow. This superficiality extends to their attempts at acting normal by exhibiting false emotions through an exaggerated affect.

- *Grandiosity:* Despite being shallow and superficial, psychopaths show no self-esteem issues. Often seen as megalomaniacs, they also have an equally overblown sense of entitlement.

- *Irresponsibility:* Psychopaths believe nothing is ever their fault. Someone else, or the world at large, is always to blame for all of their problems. This makes sense if you understand that psychopaths think themselves perfect. Nothing wrong can ever originate with them and so logic, the psychopath's logic, dictates that everything bad is always someone else's fault.

- *Impulsive Behavior:* The psychopath's impulsive behavior makes sense in light of their megalomania. In their world, whatever they want is good and whatever they do not want is bad. If a psychopath wants sex and his date will not provide it, then rape is good and the date is bad. If someone has money in his or her pocket and the psychopath wants it, then robbery is good and the victim is bad for possessing something the psychopath wanted. If a psychopath hates Black people and wants us all dead, murdering us is good and we are bad because we are Black. If this strikes you as crazier than a shithouse rat – it is.

- *Poor Behavior Control:* This characteristic can be misleading since many psychopaths exhibit excellent self-control by having to pretend to be 'Normal' for most of their lives. The lack of self-control comes into play when the megalomania causes them to do and behave exactly as they please at any time they have an urge. This brings us to the next characteristic.

- *Lacking Goals:* Another characteristic attributed to the psychopath is the lack of goals, but this can be misleading. Many psychopaths have goals, such as murder two victims at once, sabotage a co-worker, or become a cop. However, often long-term goals are subverted to short-term goals that are, as described previously, whatever the psychopath wants at that particular moment.

- *Compulsive Lying:* Lies are the premier weapon of a psychopath. Lies hold together their view of themselves, their own private universe, and facilitate their need to live parasitically off the rest of society.

  Without empathy, shame, and remorse they are free to lie as often and as outrageously as they please. Normal people would blush, or sweat, or tremble, if they dared stretch the truth to the same degree. However, for the psychopath, lying is as easy and natural as breathing. This is why they often pass polygraphs. They do not register the physiological reactions that non-psychopaths would when lying. They are so good at lying they can fool trained psychiatrists and even other psychopaths. What is important to know is that given the right circumstances they can fool ANYONE.

- *Manipulative:* Hand in hand with the psychopath's extraordinary ability to lie comes the ability to manipulate others for their own benefit. Having spent their lifetime studying us, psychopaths are masters of manipulation and experts on knowing how to push our buttons to use our emotions against us. They use this ability to keep those around them confused, unable to think clearly, and off balance.

  Psychopaths also learn very early how their personalities can have traumatizing effects on the personalities of non-psychopaths, and how to take advantage of this for purposes of achieving their goals.

- *Anti-social Behavior:* The very essence of the psychopath is anti-social. Their lack of empathy for other people extends onto society and the environment. Vandalism, pollution, animal abuse, environmental destruction, building code violations, reckless driving, and a host of morally and socially unacceptable activities are of no concern to the psychopath.

These then are the basic characteristics that psychopaths exhibit. Bear in mind that few psychopaths will express all of the characteristics, and that non-psychopaths can have many of these characteristics as well.

Common Types of Psychopaths

While there are as many variations in the personalities of psychopaths as there are among normal people, the following lists some general archetypes:

Narcissists: The most benign form of psychopathology is pathological narcissism. Narcissists are so overcome with self-love that nothing else in the world matters but them. They need a constant source of Narcissistic Supply, which is attention, adoration, recognition, awards, and praise.

There are two basic types of narcissist, the *Somatic,* and the *Cerebral.*

Somatic Narcissists take pride in their looks and appearance. They will flaunt their sexual exploits, brag of their accomplishments, show off their muscles, and display their toys. They are often health nuts, hypochondriacs and sex addicts. Much of their narcissistic supply comes from having numerous sexual partners, but the act itself, often flamboyant and exaggerated, is nonetheless merely an empty show put on by the narcissist for his or her own amusement. Because of their barren inner life, they continually need new thrills simply for the rush of adrenaline. These thrills range from criminal activity and substance abuse to increasingly bizarre sexual acts.

Cerebral Narcissists love their own minds. They are arrogant, condescending, and 'know-it-alls' that pride themselves on being smarter than everyone else is. Contrary to the somatic type, cerebral narcissists often regard their body and its maintenance as a nuisance and burden and are physically lazy, unfit, and often celibate. Their narcissistic supply comes from fame, notoriety, awards, and displays of wealth to create envy in others.

The danger to the public from narcissists is the drain on energy, time, resources, and emotional wellbeing. A narcissist is interested in a person only for what narcissistic supply that person can provide. They will gladly accept love, attention, affection, adoration, praise, emotional and financial support, but being without empathy, they cannot reciprocate any of it. Any partnership they enter into will always be one sided. Once a person ceases to be a source of narcissistic supply, or a better source comes along, they are discarded without hesitation or consideration. Thus, narcissists leave behind a trail of broken hearts, broken dreams, empty wallets, and abandoned children.

The Victim: Preying on what psychopaths see as a weakness in others, sympathy, these psychopaths appears helpless, pitiful, emotionally fragile, persecuted, and sexually vulnerable. They pretend heartfelt gratitude for whatever small kindness strangers provide them, but behind their masks are cunning, ruthless, and loveless predators. Often using sex as the hook, they can juggle several victims at a time, draining them of life and money until there is nothing left, then skipping town to avoid the repercussions.

Con Artists: Not all con artists are psychopaths, but psychopaths make convincing con artists. Being excellent liars, they put that talent to use by cheating others. Without a conscience or remorse to stand in the way, they are free to cheat old women out of their life savings, sell quack cures to terminally ill patients, or shortchange the blind. They are usually charming, articulate and convincing, and make successful salespersons. Unlike the Narcissist, the Con Artist is not as concerned about love or attention, as money.

There are two types of cons psychopaths engage in the *Short Con* and the *Big Store Con*. The Short Con is probably the one that most often comes to mind when thinking about con artists. These are tricks and cheats that require no great intelligence to pull off, such as short changing, bait and switch, and Three Card Monte to name a few.

Psychopaths that have a higher intelligence level are more likely to establish the Big Store Con. These are large-scale frauds that all rely on a basic strategy. Take something of little to no value, artificially inflate the perceived value, sell to gullible investors, take the money and run. Traditional big store cons use real estate, stocks, and bonds as the lure. Even 'reputable' multinational corporations, accounting firms, and banks are all capable of being nothing more than a large-scale con. While the short con can deprive a victim of a few to a few thousand dollars, the big store cons are especially destructive, capable of destroying an entire nation's economy.

The after effects of the these psychopaths are usually financial devastation along with all the repercussions of broken marriages, suicides, alcoholism, domestic violence, drug addiction, and ruined lives.

Monsters in Flesh: More popularly known as Anti-Social Personality Disorder, or Sociopaths, these are the real life monsters of our nightmares. These are the wife-beaters, murderers, serial killers, stalkers, rapists, sadists, pedophiles, gangsters, and terrorists. They are often cops, in the military, or career criminals.

Often showing their contempt with a sneer or smirk and with a thousand yard stare from dead eyes, they are dangerous, unpredictable, and easily triggered into violence. Cowardly and sadistic, they tend to target the most vulnerable in society – women, children, and the elderly and disabled – or they will target a specific group they hate, such as Afrikans, children, or women with red hair.

Often impulsive and opportunistic, sociopaths will not hesitate to commit any type of crime and will use manipulation, intimidation, and violence to get what they want.

The Monster in Flesh can show signs of their illness as early as age three. Early warning signs include compulsive lying, fighting, stealing, bullying, bad judgment, cheating, cruelty to animals, vandalism, truancy, sexual activity, fire-setting, substance abuse, and running away from home. The Monster in Flesh is the natural born killer.

Professional Psychopaths: The Monster in Flesh is the most dangerous; however, it is the Professional Psychopath that is the most destructive.

While the victims of the former can range in the dozens, the victims of the professional psychopath can run into the tens of millions. These psychopaths litter history with genocides and the destruction of entire nations and empires. Historical examples include such monsters as Chicago Mayor Richard J. Daley; pioneer of propaganda, Edward Bernays and Roman Emperor Gaius Julius Caesar Germanicus, better known as "Caligula." While there are many that make it to the pinnacle of the *political* arena there are also such Professional Psycopaths as J.P. Morgan, Randolph Hearst, and Mayer Rothschild, who reached the pinnacle of the *financial* arena, where they cause no less misery and destruction as their political counterparts.

The professional psychopath is just as malevolent, narcissistic, and remorseless, as the other stereotypes, they are just much smarter. They can be found in any profession but usually governments, corporations, and religions will be thick with them.

In a corporation, the professional psychopaths are ideally suited for advancement. They can masterfully fake their abilities and credentials, use their intellect and charm to manipulate and exploit others, and generally backstab their way to high positions. Once in power, their masks slip and they abuse their power and bully and sabotage their coworkers and subordinates.

In politics, the professional psychopath's ruthlessness and cunning gives them a distinct advantage over any non-psychopath rival. They make charismatic leaders, manipulating and brainwashing the naive, vulnerable, uneducated, or mentally weak. Mastery of lying allows them to make whatever outrageous campaign promises with a straight face, but, of course, with no intention of keeping any of them. A life spent faking being human gives them the ability to assume the role of the virtuous public servant, the perfect father, husband, advisor, mentor, and everyman. In addition when things get rough they have no inhibitions in playing dirty and readily resort to murder, assassination, persecution, war and genocide.

The third sphere of power that has traditionally attracted more than its fair share of psychopaths is religion. A quick glance at the tortures of the Spanish Inquisitions, and the seemingly endless religious wars waged in the name of peace and love makes their influence plainly visible to all willing to look. In most religions, compulsive liars make the perfect proselytizers. A look at recently created religions such as Mormonism and Scientology show their founders, Joseph Smith and L. Ron Hubbard respectively, were at least compulsive liars, and more likely full-blown psychopaths. Charismatic cult leaders such as Jim Jones and Sun Myung Moon were indeed psychopaths, while televangelist preachers that rake in millions from their gullible flocks are, at best, con artists of the highest caliber.

Religions' moral education and veils of 'goodness' attract psychopaths that use their membership in the religion as a cover, an extra sugar-coating, lest anyone suspect their true nature.

When psychopaths dominate and seize control of the major cultural institutions that influence a society, a final type of psychopath is created:

Secondary Psychopaths: While the classic psychopath is one who is born with whatever genetic trait that causes this pathology, there is another group of people that behave just like the classic psychopath who were NOT born that way but were *created*.

Secondary psychopaths are created in two ways, through *trauma* and through *groups*.

Trauma from an accident, drug addiction, or severe physical and psychological abuse can destroy that part of the brain's frontal cortex where empathy and conscience is processed. While such individuals are a tragic reality in our society, they are in most cases just as incurable as their genetic counterparts are. The exception is in drug induced psychopathy. Most drug addicts will behave like psychopaths since the criminality of their addiction forces them to adopt psychopathy as a psychological survival mechanism. With drug rehabilitation, they may regain their conscience, provided the drug use did not severely damage the brain itself.

The second way in which psychopaths are created is through groups. There are certain groups that will attract psychopaths because of the opportunities of power and influence membership provides. Usually such groups will quickly become led and dominated by psychopaths. Other non-psychopathic members of these groups would have to become psychopaths in order to survive.

For example, on police forces in America, sociopaths make the best leaders and therefore most police departments have a sociopath at its head. Other psychopaths are also attracted to the violence and power of a police force and so together they create a psychopathic value system. The police force becomes a psychopathic entity. The non-psychopathic brother or sister who joins such a force – whether they are trying to be "the Spook who Sat by the Door" or whether they believe they can change the system from within – must adopt the group's twisted value system and behave accordingly, thus they become a secondary psychopath.

At the other end of the scale, we can see the same principle at work in corporations. The money and power of a corporation attracts the cerebral and narcissistic psychopaths. In a corporate environment they have many advantages over their non-psychopathic competitors for promotion. Not surprisingly, most corporations end up being run by psychopaths. As with a police force, a corporation's culture adopts the twisted values of its leaders. Those who would seek employment must likewise adopt or at least *appear* to adopt the corporation's essentially psychopathic mindset.

What is important to understand is that a mob has no conscience. Individual members may or may not have a conscience but when they are part of a mob, they will have none. Police forces, major corporations and even some street organizations are mobs. It would be a mistake to place your trust in them since they can turn predatory in a moment and deprive you of time, money, sanity and livelihood.

The Psychopath's Modus Operandi

One weakness psychopaths have is that once you study them and begin to understand them, they become predictable.

While *tactics* vary from one to another, most psychopaths follow a similar *strategy* when conning either an individual or an organization. Their strategy is as follows:

The Interview: Psychopaths are experts at *Cold Reading.* 'Cold Reading' is the ability to guess a person's personality type quickly through verbal and non-verbal communication. The technique is simple, ask questions and watch the responses. Psychopaths will Cold Read you as part of what is called the *interview stage.* The whole purpose of the interview is for the psychopath to size you up as a potential victim. They make mental notes of different ways they could possibly manipulate you.

Learning to say less and observe more when first meeting people is the easiest way to defend against a psychopath. In social situations, be congenial without revealing personal information that could be used against you later.

Remember that getting to know you is a privilege that should be earned over time.

The Seduction: Should *the interview* reveal that you or your organization is a suitable victim, the next stage is *the seduction*. Based on the results of their interview, the psychopath will tailor the seduction to your personality. If you are concerned about your appearance, they will flatter your good looks; if you are insecure about your level of education, they will flatter you about your intelligence. If you are greedy, they will have insider information on a get-rich-quick scheme.

On a personal level, they will shower you with praise and attention in a whirlwind "romance." They make sure that being around them is fun and exciting so that you become addicted to the adrenalin rush they create.

On the organizational level, they pretend to be the perfect employee, the most devout follower, the most dedicated public servant. They work to ingratiate themselves first to the gatekeepers, and finally the power holders, often by being shameless sycophants and boot lickers.

Pay close attention to how everyone who is in your personal space or organization came in and how they move up in the ranks.

Divide and Conquer: Just as a hunting pride of lionesses will seek to separate a targeted antelope from the rest of the herd, so psychopaths seek to isolate their victims from the rest of humanity. They accomplish this through the strategy of *divide and conquer*.

In a personal relationship, the psychopath will sabotage and undermine his or her victim's relationships with family and friends. They tell you that if your family and friends don't believe as you do, stop dealing with them; they tell you that our "unconscious" brothers and sisters should be avoided altogether while claiming to love Afrikan people –as if the so-called unconscious brothers and sisters are not just as Afrikan.

Either the victim leaves their "lost" family members and friends alone, or, exasperated by the negative drama and costs associated with the victim, their friends and family drop out of contact, leaving the victim without the support and guidance of their social group.

In an organizational setting, psychopaths are the consummate office politicians. They seek to create factions within the organization and then turn those factions against each other to create as much chaos as possible. In this instance, the psychopath is called an *agent provocateur*.

Psychopaths swim in chaos; the more, the better. Secretly, they start to draw the gullible, weak minded, and fellow psychopaths to their side while intensifying their efforts to have the most talented, honest, and incorruptible members – ones that could have the strength of character to expose them, expelled. They poison the environment in a variety of ways so that everyone feels irritable, edgy, and unable to perform their jobs. Control of the organization slips into the hands of the source behind the dysfunction: the agent provocateur who created it all.

At this stage, the only defense is to flee the situation. You cannot win this battle since the psychopath's ruthlessness will trump any counter attack you could conceive of. By the time you smell the smoke, the psychopath has already stolen the fire extinguishers.

If you are in a personal relationship with such a psychopath, cut your losses and run. In an organization, find a new job; in a nation, become an expatriate.

Fear and Tyranny: The final stage of the psychopath's strategy is tyranny – the absolute and sadistic control over his victims.

In a relationship, the honeymoon is over and the mask comes off. The psychopath suddenly becomes controlling, abusive, and violent. Instead of flattery and attention, the tactics are now fear, intimidation, extortion, and emotional blackmail.

On the organizational level, you see benefits being cut, while time cards, production quotas, and surveillance increases. Employees become slaves; powerless and disposable cogs in a machine run for the sole benefit of the psychopaths in charge.

On the national level, countries ruled by psychopaths become corrupt and brutish police states constantly at war with created and imaginary enemies. The population becomes paranoid, neurotic, and ultimately secondary psychopaths. In a psychopathic culture, everyone must adopt a ruthless attitude as a survival strategy. The United States of America is a psychopathic nation and anyone patriotic to this bastard nation has become a secondary psychopath.

At this stage there is little chance to flee and escape safely. Instead, you may be left with few options other than to tough it out and fight, hope for rescue or pray for the psychopaths to die. Personally, I don't seek saviors and I'm not much of a praying man, so I am left with but one option.

Defense Against The Psychopath

Belief in Monsters: One of the greatest advantages psychopaths have is that average, decent people cannot believe that such monsters truly exist.

This inability to comprehend the predator mentality is partly due to popular morality. We have learned simplistic and idealistic morality through schools and churches that teach such platitudes as all men are created equal, everyone has some good in them, everyone is special, and so forth. Such ideals serve as a cover that the true machinations of society can operate behind without evoking our suspicion.

Another reason that people cannot face evil is fear. The true nature of psychopaths is the stuff of childhood nightmares. Many people simply cannot deal with the fear this causes, so to soothe their nerves, they revert to an infantile strategy of denial and magical thinking:

"If I don't acknowledge the existence of monsters, then the monsters can't hurt me."

Okay, don't acknowledge the existence of speeding cars as you stand in the middle of a highway dressed in black at night and see how that turns out for you.

The first line of defense against psychopaths is acknowledging their existence. By doing so, you develop a psychological advantage. Forewarned is forearmed and having braced yourself with the knowledge of predatory individuals, you are better able to think clearly and thus spot the predator before he can spot you.

Once you accept the reality that human predators populate our society, the next line of defense is in identifying them. Because of their abilities at camouflage and deception, psychopaths are difficult to spot. They can fool even mental health professionals. It is important to understand that everyone can be conned. If you feel you are the exception, you only make yourself more susceptible.

Recognition: A psychopath is like a smoking ember. The sooner you can spot the smoke and douse the ember the better, since after the house is on fire it is too late to contain the damage and destruction. Learn to spot the typical psychopathic character traits, and recognize their modus operandi.

Where possible, do background checks and/or speak with the suspected psychopath's family and friends. Most psychopaths leave a long trail of destruction and heartbreak and will try to cover their tracks. A lack of background information is just as suspicious as a history of betrayals, by the way.

Another fundamental flaw psychopaths possess is a lack of patience and the incredible energy they use to maintain their façade. Over time, they drop their masks. Thus, one of the best methods of detecting psychopaths is to wait them out.

Once you identify someone as being a psychopath you have only two options: attack or evade; strike or fade.

What NOT To Do

What is vital to understand is that empathy cannot defeat the psychopath. You cannot change them, you cannot reform them, you cannot find the goodness inside them, you cannot show them the way to God, and you cannot teach them about love. All these approaches are doomed to failure since psychopaths can never understand nor can they care about these concepts.

While they may lead you to believe that you are getting through to them, in reality, your empathy infuriates them and, far from admiring your compassion, they despise you even more.

While you try to understand the psychopath, they are secretly calculating how best to cause you the most suffering. You must develop a cold exterior to them and view them from a distance. Do not pity them, feel sorry for them, or sympathize with them.

Attack: Should you feel no other recourse but to confront a psychopath, your one advantage is their fear of being exposed for what they are. They have known since childhood that they are different from most people. Their whole advantage lies in the fact that they know what they are and no one else does. Exposing a psychopath takes away his or her advantage and reveals their inner corruption for all to see. However, few people have the strength and intelligence to do this successfully. While the statistical distribution of genius and idiot psychopaths mirrors the general population, even a moronic psychopath can elude and outwit an educated accuser.

Before you attempt to expose and expunge a psychopath you must be in a position of power, and you must choose the time and place. You also need to have your people briefed and ready to support you. This means creating a family and friends support group and/or joining a support group. In an organizational setting you need to have coworkers, managers, the legal department, and human resources on your side before making your move.

It is best not to corner a psychopath, since the fight will likely be more vicious than most people can bear. Instead, use the threat of exposure to drive the psychopath away. The thought that they could be exposed at any time is unnerving and most psychopaths will give up the current game and go in search of more ignorant and vulnerable prey.

In an organization, you may have to offer not to expose the psychopath to the press and/or to the community if the psychopath will simply resign and never come back.

Evade: A safer and easier strategy is to evade the psychopath. Once you have identified someone as a psychopath, you must cut him or her off and out of your life completely. In a relationship, you may need to change your locks, change your phone numbers, block your e-mail account, close bank accounts, or move. Do not tip your hand that you are leaving and take self-defense and firearms training, just in case.

CHAPTER TWO
LIES & DECEPTION

Deception is one of the fundamental strategies of nature. From camouflage to impersonation, the ability to deceive has been an advantage to survival. Modern man has taken this lesson to heart. Our ability to deceive has outstripped our ability to *detect* deception, which gives liars the advantage.

The best defense against liars is to be able to tell when they are lying. Unfortunately, there is no fool proof method for doing so. Even a polygraph or 'Lie Detector' is far from accurate, but by understanding the principles behind the polygraph we can get a better understanding of why it is so difficult to discern truth from falsehood.

A polygraph uses sensors to record four physiological reactions and transcribe that information in the form of a graph. The reactions monitored are respiration, heart rate, blood pressure, and skin resistance. The theory is that when a person is lying, he or she will inwardly feel anxiety, guilt, and fear, which will in turn trigger an increase in respiration, heart rate, blood pressure, and skin perspiration (known as the *Galvanic Skin Response*). However, there are three situations where lie detectors fail to give an accurate assessment.

First, most people become anxious when they are questioned or interrogated. Their anxiety may be misread as lying, when in fact it is fear of not being believed. This is known as the *Othello Effect* – the readings indicate fear rather than guilt. While professional interviewers are aware of this and adjust their methods to compensate, it is nevertheless more art than science; hence the polygraphs' limited viability in the judicial system.

Second, lie detectors don't work on psychopaths. Without a conscience, there is no guilt, and no anxiety that would cause physiological changes. It is natural for normal people to feel some anxiety when being questioned; therefore it is the confident and smooth answers that should raise warning flags.

Third, a lie detector cannot tell what is true or false, but only what a person *believes* is true and false. If a person believes he/she is telling the truth, even if it is false, the detector will still indicate that the person was being truthful. The best liars are those that believe their own lies.

In addition, a person can learn to control those physiological reactions that a polygraph monitors through simple biofeedback exercises. Even a person with a conscience can be easily trained to pass a polygraph.

Keeping the above drawbacks in mind, one can duplicate some of the information gathered by mechanical lie detectors through careful observation. Remember that these observations are of discomfort, fear, and doubt – reactions that may or may not be caused by guilt. No one indicator is sufficient to base a judgment on. You must observe the overall behavior and responses, test the logic, and base judgment on your own experience.

Non-Verbal Clues To Deception

Nonverbal clues include movements and gestures that may indicate an inner conflict. Known as *Body Langauge* and *Non-verbal Communication*, knowledge of man's peculiar physical quirks have been around for ages. In the martial arts, body langauge that reveals an opponent's next move is called *telegraphing*. In gambling, a gesture that reveals whether a person is bluffing or not is known as the *tell*. Below are common ways in which people's gestures may reveal deception:

The Eyes: One way in which the eyes reveal inner emotions are through pupil dilation. The eyes' pupils control the amount of light that passes through the lens of the eye by contracting under bright lighting conditions, and dilating under low. Pupil dilation is also an indication of increased brain processing. The brain processes more information when thinking over a problem and when aroused or excited. This is why dilated pupils are thought to show desire.

Pupil dilation also indicates when a person is lying. This is because lying is a more complex process than telling the truth. To tell the truth is simply memory recall, while *lying requires both memory of the truth, and memory of the lie used to cover the truth.* As lies multiply, the process becomes more and more complex. As a result, the pupils tend to dilate more when someone is lying.

Along with dilation, the rate at which a person blinks will also increase when excited or aroused by visual stimuli. Blink-rate is the number of times the eyes blink in a minute. When excited, blinking increases. When viewing unpleasant material, and when concentrating, the blink rate slows down and staring occurs more often. Examples can be found in the flirtatious batting of the eyes, and in the horrified stares of victims of violence. Increased blink rate during questioning may indicate that the topic is creating anxiety.

The final clue the eyes reveal is one that almost everyone seems to know – that when hiding something, we tend to avoid eye contact. This clue is so universally known that professional liars know to look you straight in the eye every time they lie. However, because this indicator is so universally faked, it is a suspect gesture. If someone looks you in the eye and tells you something that still does not feel right, it probably is not.

Hand Gestures: Man's first form of communication was probably a hand langauge based on the simple gestures the hands make when performing specific functions. For example, holding one hand, palm up, under the mouth while scooping toward the mouth with the other hand is universally recognized as the symbol for eating.

Travelers, immigrants, and tourists still use hand gestures to communicate when no one can speak the same langauge. This langauge is so embedded in our psyches that even when speaking, our bodies echo our verbal langauge with accompanying gestures. While the mouth can lie, the body seldom does.

Subconsciously, we sense that if we use our hands when lying, the actions may not fit our words and so the use of hand gestures decreases when someone is lying.

Another common gesture using the hands that may indicate lying is a touching of the mouth or face. The hand begins toward the mouth as if subconsciously they want to stop the lie from being spoken. Since this is too obvious, the hand is redirected to the cheeks, chin, eyes, or forehead. The closer the hand comes to the mouth the greater the lie.

Body Gestures: When a person is lying, they tend to increase their use of the shrug gesture and raised eyebrows. Using this gesture is a way of saying "I don't know," or "My name's Bennett...and I ain't *in* it!" This is an attempt to distance themselves from the lies they are telling. The shrug is always a negative gesture to what the person is saying.

Another indicator of lying is a restless shifting or squirming, as though the body wanted to escape. Most people control this urge to move but even still, the body will tend to make subtle movements. The restless tapping of a foot, bouncing knee, or rapping of the fingers on a tabletop are usually indicators that a person is uncomfortable with the subject matter.

Voice: Natural speech is more than words alone; it consists of auditory tones, rhythms, and cadences. An indicator of how important rhythm and tone are to communication can be seen in those suffering from a rare brain disorder known as *aphasia*. With aphasia, the portion of the brain that processes verbal word meanings is inoperative. As a result, *aphasics* – those with this disorder – develop an enhanced ability to detect a "feeling tone" that enables them to recognize when someone is lying. While the average person cannot detect the subtle nuances of another's voice like an aphasic, we can listen for certain clues.

When under stress, people speak a little higher than normal and there is a tendency for the voice to break and become raspy. Voice level or volume lowers when saying things the speaker would rather not say.

If a person is uncertain or nervous about his answers, he may incorporate a rising 'question' tone in his speech especially on the last word of each sentence. This tone is similar to the tone used when asking a question such as 'who?' only less pronounced.

Speech patterns change when people lie. There is a tendency not to use contractions. For example, "I didn't do it" is more believable then "I did not do it." The latter is an indication the speech is carefully thought out, rather than flowing spontaneously. Other clues that indicate a person is thinking out his answers are false starts – the person starts with one explanation and suddenly changes to something else – and frequent pauses and stalling vocalizations: the "ahs" and "umms" between sentences.

Physiological Clues*:* A polygraph measures physiological changes caused by the fear and shame a normal person would feel when lying. Fear triggers the *Flight or Flight* response in the sympathetic nervous system, which increases blood pressure, respiration, perspiration, and heart rate. Some of these effects are visible to the careful observer. These include, increased breath rate, sweating, blushing, a vein that begins to throb on the face, forehead, or neck, and a trembling in the hands or jaw.

Logical Clues to Deception

When examining information that seems suspicious, look for contradictions in logic such as timeframe, continuity, and probabilities.

Contradiction in Time-line*:* Unless you have actually experienced a particular activity or event, it would be unlikely that you would know what timetable that event or activity followed. By questioning other witnesses or experts in that field, you can get an approximate timetable and compare it to that given by the suspect. For example, your teenaged son or daughter says they were at the library until ten, but you find out the library closed at nine. Another mistake in time-line is expanding or contracting time, either too much occurred in too short a time, or not enough occurred in too long a time.

Recently, a brother told me he was a combat medic in the 5th Special Forces Group. I asked his MOS (Military Occupational Specialty; i.e. "job"). He paused and then said "My MOS? It was 96 Charlie." I knew he was lying – all Special Forces MOS designations begin with 18. I believe he was telling the truth about his MOS, though – all 96, 97 and 98 are all Military Intelligence. A 96 Charlie is a Counter Intelligence Specialist, the army's counterpart to an FBI/Homeland Security agent.

Contradiction in Continuity: This is where a person knows something he should not have knowledge of, or does not know something he should. This tactic is used in criminal investigations by keeping secret certain details about a crime. Then when questioning a suspect, investigators watch to see if he reveals knowledge of such details, details that only the guilty party would know. Another ancient tactic is to pretend not to know some piece of information that you have already verified, and see if the person's answers match the information you know to be true.

Contradictions in Procedure: Every job and occupation follows rules and procedures. Anyone describing events that are contrary to the standard procedures are likely giving false witness unless there is a logical reason why those procedures were not being followed. If Sandra Bland really committed suicide in police custody, where are the indicators that she was suicidal? On the other hand, if the claims by police *to protect and serve* the people are sincere why are they utilizing training and carrying weapons formerly used only by the military?

The most obvious flaw is when something is too good to be true, the solution too easy, and the answer too simple. Age and experience teach that nothing worthwhile is easy, or simple.

Behavioral Clues To Deception

When someone is accused of a misdeed, there are three possible responses: redirection, confrontation, and examination.

Redirection: If a person's initial response to an accusation is to blame someone else, he or she is either immature, or has a guilty conscience. This is the tactic children use when accused of a misdeed. – "It wasn't me, it was Oluade!"

A variation of this is to insist that because some other parties are involved or committed similar transgressions therefore the individual's guilt is absolved – "Abiola did it, too!"

Another form of redirection is mock assistance in finding the "true culprit" by proposing alternate theories and scenarios.

Confrontation: When the accused responds with indignation and counter charges it may be genuine, or a ruse to draw attention away from the accusation and place the focus onto the accusers or on the victim. This is a common strategy used by the press whom, after an Afrikan is murdered by the police, rather than dwell on the question of the cop's guilt or innocence, attack the character of the victim.

Investigation: When wrongly accused, innocent people are interested in exposing the truth because the truth is obviously on their side. They will want to examine details since, by careful investigation, the truth of their innocence is revealed. The guilty however would prefer to gloss-over the details and try to block any investigation. More often the guilty are revealed through their cover-up of evidence rather than the actual evidence itself.

Learning and applying these simple observations to the people you are dealing with will not allow you to spot *all* deceptions but it will raise a red flag when something is suspicious.

CHAPTER THREE
ANGER & AGGRESSION

The highest level of self-defense is the *avoidance* of conflict – to influence the course of events in order to dissipate the conflict before it arises. You win the battle without drawing your sword.

To accomplish this strategy it is important to understand the causes of – and recognize the behavior patterns associated with – *anger* and *aggression*.

Causes of Aggression

Among animals and humans, aggressive behaviors are caused by the following factors.

Territory: People can become irritable and aggressive if they feel their territory has been threatened or invaded. Each person stakes out and defends several territories. These are:

- ***Intimate Space****:* An imaginary shell extending from the surface of the skin to a distance of four to six inches. This space is reserved for family, and close friends. Only under special conditions are strangers allowed to enter this space, such as doctors, therapists, and sports coaches.

- **Personal Space**: Personal Space extends beyond intimate space another two to three feet depending on cultural norms. For example, the British prefer dealing with strangers at arm's length, while Arabs are accustomed to closer interaction – at elbow's length. Personal space is shared with friends, co-workers, and family. A stranger entering personal space makes most people feel uncomfortable even if not considered a threat.

- **Home Territory**: Is the area where you live. The boundaries of a person's personal living area are proportionate to the person's economic status within a particular society. A homeless person's home territory may extend no further than the space of a sleeping bag, while, at the other end of the spectrum, the home territory of financial moguls can extend to miles. The people and possessions found within a home territory are also considered the property of the estate. A mate is "territory" and will be defended against the threat of other suitors, likewise children are defended against strangers, and possessions defended against theft.

- **The Hunting Grounds**: Any area that provides enough resources to survive on can be a hunting ground. For hunting and gathering societies, the hunting ground is the amount of territory needed to provide enough game and edible plants to feed the tribe. For pastoral groups the hunting ground would consist of enough grassland to feed their flocks, likewise a farmer's hunting grounds are his fields and so on. In the urban environment, the hunting ground can be the office, factory, storefront or street corner. Executives claim an office, corporations claim a market share, police claim a beat, street organizations claim a neighborhood, and low-level drug dealers claim a street corner. The boundaries are different, but the instinct is the same.

Inter-Male: Some aggressive behavior is present in *all* group interaction as a means of establishing group hierarchy. This type of aggression is used to dominate rivals within the group, thereby establishing a pecking order. The animal able to dominate all the others becomes the leader, the animal able to dominate all but the leader, becomes second in the chain of command and so on. Confrontations motivated by inter-male aggression usually end the moment one of the rivals withdraws or displays submissive behavior. They seldom end in actual violence.

Leadership goes to the most aggressive. In war, this is usually the strongest and bravest; in society, it is often the loudest and most brazen.

Sex Related: Aggression is also a component in the competition for mating partners. All animals have the instinct to compete with each other for mates to ensure species survival through genetic diversity.

Those unable to compete for a mate may be sick or have some genetic flaw that would thus be bred out of the species.

In humans, you can observe similar behavior by placing an attractive woman among a group of men. Almost immediately, men of breeding age begin to strut and posture more aggressively, talk louder and gestures become more exaggerated. Each man, consciously or not, is competing for the woman's attention by showing off his health, vigor, and machismo, the human equivalent of a gorilla beating his chest. With primates and humans alike, the most dominant males have the most mating partners.

Fear Induced: It could be argued that all forms of aggression are the result of fear. Fear of losing what you have or not getting what you want, fear of others, and fear of death. Another reason may lie within the brain itself. Pain, fear, and aggression are regulated by the limbic system. Stimulation of one of these functions may cause a crossover stimulation of the other functions so that pain induces fear and fear induces aggression.

Maternal/Paternal: Maternal aggression is the instinctive defense of offspring against real or perceived threats. As a result, new mothers have a heightened sense of territoriality. They are also more likely to interpret anyone entering their territory as a threat, and are more likely to respond with greater than normal aggression.

Irritability: There are a number of factors that will increase irritable aggression such as hunger, thirst, exhaustion, discomfort, frustration, worry, and pain.

Alcohol And Drugs: Scientists and nonscientists alike have long recognized the association between alcohol consumption and aggressive behavior.

Alcohol weakens brain mechanisms that normally restrain impulsive behaviors, including inappropriate aggression. By impairing information processing, alcohol can also lead a person to misjudge social cues, thereby overreacting to a perceived threat. Simultaneously, a narrowing of attention may lead to an inaccurate assessment of the future risks of acting on an immediate violent impulse.

Many drugs such as cocaine and methamphetamines have similar effects and in addition to promoting aggression, paranoia and violence, can even trigger psychotic episodes. One should always be aware that people under the influence of these substances are more likely to be aggressive and violent.

Based on published studies, up to 86 percent of homicide offenders, 37 percent of assault offenders, 60 percent of sexual offenders, up to 57 percent of men and 27 percent of women involved in marital violence, and 13 percent of child abusers were drinking at the time of the offense.

Predatory: In many circumstances, aggressive behavior is rewarded, and is therefore more likely to occur. In environments where resources are scarce, aggression ensures survival.

In such an environment, children learn to grab what they can, when they can, or else do without. This applies first to food and attention, then, as children become adults, to mating partners, money, jobs, status, and power.

In poor and overcrowded environments, only those who fiercely pursue their goals, allowing nothing and no one to get in their way, have any chance of attaining them. Thus, aggression becomes an instrument, a method to achieve goals and gain rewards.

Signs of Aggression

Animals settle disputes with what is called *Threat Display Behavior* – showing the teeth, puffing up, raising the hair and other actions designed to make the animal look fierce and formidable. Rarely do animals of the same species come to blows and even when they do, the fighting is more symbolic than lethal.

Humans also use threatening displays to intimidate rivals. Like animals, when human rivals come to blows, the injuries are usually minor. It is usually when men are in groups that serious injuries or deaths occur.

Nations also use threat display behavior by staging war games and practicing maneuvers near the borders of rival nations. This is also known as sword rattling.

Before hostilities devolve into open violence, you can usually recognize some of the following behaviors indicative of aggressive intent:

Posturing: Like many species, humans attempt to make themselves appear bigger and more fearsome than they really are. This is done by puffing up and expanding the chest, letting the arms hang away from the body and spreading the legs. To appear fiercer men walk with a swagger, often thrusting the head forwards.

Staring: The stare is a universal signal that can indicate either sexual or physical aggression.

Gesturing: Anger stimulates the sympathetic nervous system that triggers the *Fight or Flight* response. If the person does not attack or flee, the energy level will rise to intolerable levels and must be dissipated through what is known as displacement behavior. In humans, this behavior takes the form of mock combat such as sharp, sudden movements – often called *bucking*, punching the air or inanimate objects, jumping and stomping the feet, throwing things, threats, making loud noises, yelling and screaming.

These are the signals for raging anger. When a person is less angry or suppressing his anger, the symptoms are similar, just less pronounced. Instead of grimacing, there may be a facial tick or a scowling gesture. Instead of a wide eyed stare, a reduction in the blink-rate. Stomping the feet becomes a tapping of the foot, punching the air becomes a rapping of the fingers.

To recognize the danger signals of imminent attack look for the following:

- profuse sweating
- rapid deep breathing
- red face
- thin lips drawn back in a grimace or scowl
- bulging eyes and intense stare
- clenched fists
- rapid cutting movements
- blowing up in size to appear larger

If dealing with a person exhibiting these signs, stay calm and appear non-threatening. Stay discreetly out of range of getting "stole on" (a "sucker punch"), slowly back away and prepare for a charge.

Preventing Anger

Everyone will lose his or her temper from time to time without really meaning to cause harm. This is a part of the human condition. People may be angry with you even if you did nothing wrong or posed no threat. The following are strategies to deal with the occasional angry outbursts from others.

Become Like Water: This works against angry outbursts by calmly absorbing and dissipating the anger. If someone is yelling, do not interrupt. Allow the person to vent his or her anger until its energy has been exhausted.

Trying to stop the anger or running away only bottles up the anger. Listen calmly and do not respond immediately to every accusation.

Angry people expect others to go on the defensive and are therefore prepared to press the attack. By remaining calm, you will prevent the conflict from escalating into a vicious circle of mutual recrimination. Eventually the person's anger will subside.

When the anger has been expressed and the person is waiting for a reply, deliberately lower your voice and speak calmly, this forces the other person to tone down their voice in order to hear what you are saying.

Ask the person what you can do to help solve the problem. This shows your concern, which reinforces the person's self-esteem.

Afterwards you may calmly agree or disagree on some of the points outlined, so that the person feels he or she is taken seriously and saves face.

Feeding anger with more anger is a waste of time that can never accomplish anything positive and is a drain on your resources of time and energy.

Stay Calm: It is a myth that repressing anger causes it to be bottled up inside only to eventually explode into violence. Research shows just the opposite. The non-expression of anger, and redirection into non-destructive activities, is indicative of intelligence and self-discipline.

Anger and aggression are learned behaviors; it controls us only because we learned to let it, we can also unlearn it.

Another reason to learn to control your temper is that enraging the enemy is a well-known military strategy. This tactic works because an angry opponent cannot think clearly, an inexcusable mistake in any situation where a rational assessment of the situation is required.

History records thousands of battles where commanders lost control and charged off to their deaths, dooming their men and country with them. You should not allow personal feelings to put yourself at such a disadvantage.

When you feel you may be on the verge of losing your temper follow these steps:

1. Stop what you are doing.

2. Breathe in slowly and deeply for three seconds, hold the breath for six seconds, and then exhale slowly for 12 seconds.

3. Relax your face and shoulders. Loosen up.

4. Count to ten – a cliché that actually works.

If this does not calm you down, then leave the situation, go for a walk, exercise, or engage in some other physical activity that will dissipate the excess energy.

Much of the anger and aggression we encounter are the result of the pressures and stress of living in crowded and highly competitive environments. Understanding the causes and recognizing the signals, one can avoid much of the senseless hostility that stalks our personal jungles.

CHAPTER FOUR
FEAR

Fear is nature's guardian that warns and alerts us to real or perceived dangers. Knowledge of fear is essential to survival since fear can sabotage our ultimate weapon – *our intelligence* – making years of self-defense and emergency survival training useless. This is why understanding how to train our response to fear is one of the most important survival skills.

Fear of a real or imagined threat triggers the autonomic nervous system to prepare the human organism for sudden and frantic activity. Known as the *Fight or Flight* response, this survival mechanism prepares the body to either, flee a potential predator through the hazards of open terrain in a race for survival, or to face the predator in a life or death battle.

Either way, the body must be able to call on every ounce of energy and numb any pain that might interfere with running or fighting.

The *autonomic nervous system* consists of the *sympathetic* and the *parasympathetic* nervous systems. The *sympathetic* nervous system is responsible for preparing the body for action, while the *parasympathetic* nervous system is responsible for preserving energy.

A threat will cause the sympathetic nervous system to signal the *endocrine* system to release hormones, causing a series of reactions:

- Increased heart rate, which increases the flow of blood throughout the body

- Respiration is affected either by hyperventilating or holding in the breath

- Arteries dilate to increase blood flow to the surface to provide the anticipated demand of oxygen from the muscles. This can be observed by the face becoming flushed

- Body temperature increases, producing sweat, and body hair may become erect

- Blood flow to the digestive organs is restricted to provide more blood to the muscles; the stomach may suddenly feel nauseous, and vomiting is not uncommon

In addition, the adrenal glands increase the availability of blood sugar (glucose) to release stored energy. This process is akin to revving the engine and feeding nitrous oxide into the fuel mixture. Endorphins, whose molecular structure closely resembles morphine, are released into the brain to numb the anticipated pain of injuries and fatigue.

However, the body cannot maintain this heightened state of readiness for long. Soon the parasympathetic system is triggered into action to counter all the changes caused by the sympathetic system: Heart rate is reduced, breathing becomes shallow, gasping, with frequent sighing, and the mouth becomes dry. Blood is drawn in towards the inner body restricting the flow to the brain, which may cause dizziness, spots in peripheral vision, and fainting. The face becomes pale and waxy and body temperature drops. The digestive system may suddenly kick in resulting in a bowel movement or release of the bladder.

For a short period, the two systems alternate back and forth in a battle for control of the body's nervous system – a battle always won, in the end, by the *parasympathetic* nervous system. All these opposing responses can take place in a matter of minutes.

Fear prepares the body for action. The accompanying increase in strength, pain threshold, and endurance can be lifesaving assets. It is a natural signal that alerts us to the threat of great bodily harm or death that we cannot do without.

However, the fear we manufacture – called worry – turns to panic and it is then that fear becomes a liability.

The problem exists not in erasing fear (or worry) entirely, but rather a delicate balance of enhanced awareness and body readiness, combined with a detached self-control. There are three quick techniques to help you lessen fear:

Breath Control: Fear triggers the instinct to make as little noise as possible and focus on the possible threat. This instinct was a benefit to our ancient ancestors huddled in the Central Afrikan bush and hearing a twig snap in the darkness, signaling an approaching predator. To make as little noise as possible, we do two things: we freeze, and we hold our breath.

To reduce noise made by the respiratory system, we either hold our breath or breathe shallowly. However, holding the breath for too long while the sympathetic nervous system is stimulated causes a sudden demand for oxygen. The signal to breathe is overstated and, instead of regular breathing, a person may begin to hyperventilate.

Hyperventilating reduces the amount of carbon dioxide (CO_2) in the bloodstream. The body needs a certain amount of CO_2 and a rapid drop of it constricts blood flow to many vital organs. Constriction of blood vessels in the brain will cause dizziness, disorientation, and may lead to loss of consciousness. Reduced blood flow to the heart muscle may lead to chest pains. The high oxygen level can make you nervous and edgy, and can cause a feeling of "pins and needles," muscle spasms, nervous twitches, and even convulsions. The effect of a lack of CO_2 also contributes to panic attacks.

Breath control is the best technique to reduce fear. Simply being aware of the tendency to hold your breath when frightened will help you establish normal breathing rhythms.

Whenever you feel frightened or anxious you should establish a regular deep breathing pattern. Focus on your abdomen and take three short breaths holding each for one second before exhaling. On the fourth breath, begin deep breathing at a medium tempo. Inhale as slowly as possible up to a count of five, then hold the breath in for a count of twice the inhalation count, and then exhale for a count of four times the inhalation count. Thus, if you breathe in for 3 seconds, hold four 6 seconds and breathe out for 12 seconds.

Abdominal breathing will help you remain calm and reduce feelings of fear.

An old home remedy to treat hyperventilation is to breath into a paper bag. We breathe out more carbon dioxide than oxygen so after a couple of breaths, the air in the paper bag will contain more carbon dioxide which in turn will be inhaled back into the lungs and help balance the oxygen/CO_2 levels and return breathing to normal.

Caution: Medical conditions, like asthma and heart attacks, can be confused with hyperventilation. In such cases, reducing oxygen and increasing carbon dioxide can be deadly.

Relax

The instinct to freeze when frightened results in tense muscles which will interfere with natural reactions and add to the anxiety by reinforcing fear, which, in turn, will result in tenser muscles, and so on, in a vicious cycle.

To break this loop you need to relax and loosen up. The first place to start is with the shoulders. Most people will raise their shoulders and pull their chins in when frightened. Pull your shoulders down and relax the muscles of the neck and shoulders. Do a couple of quick shoulder and neck rolls then shake out your arms and hands. Pull your head up and chin out. This posture is associated with confidence and will help dispel anxiety.

Movement

The instinct to freeze when frightened is epitomized in the metaphor of a deer caught in the headlights. Startled by a car traveling down the road, a deer will often freeze in the middle of the road to its demise rather than run off into the safety of the bush. Likewise, many people will also freeze into inaction during a threatening situation. To break this instinct, you should simply move.

Rather than just wait in dread, go into action. Either go to the rescue or evacuate the scene. Doing *something* will lessen the dread of fear and help to restore confidence.

Whether you are in an accident, natural disaster or predatory attack, remember to breathe, relax, and take action to ensure your – and your family's – safety.

Overcoming Worry

We all know the feeling of being terrified about an upcoming event – a dance recital; a lecture before a large crowd; sparring in a martial arts tournament. Your palms sweat, your heart pounds and your mind races. We often confuse this feeling with fear, but it is not. It is *worry* – fear we manufacture. You are not in any danger of great bodily harm or death, so you know it is not fear.

Fear is constructive; worry is destructive. If fear is to be overcome, then you KNOW worry *must* be.

Warriors learn to manage their emotions and create an aura of invincibility even when they are scared to death. You can emulate and adapt these methods into your daily life too. Here are 3 simple tricks for building courage – acting despite your fear or worry:

Scripting: The method warriors use to solidify their game plan and to stick to it.

Warriors take inventory of their strengths and weaknesses and those of their enemy. This intelligence gathering helps them to fine-tune a *script*.

If you are going into a situation such as an important interview or blind date, do a little research about the people you will come into contact with and their affiliations and then script a dialogue in your head that consists of questions and answers that might become part of the conversation.

In order to be truly successful, warriors must instill the script into *bodily memory*, much like a method actor embeds the dialogue of a play or movie into his or her entire being.

Put yourself in the situation over and over again, so that nothing is new to you. That way, you don't panic; you are comfortable.

Fully embodying the script will make you more confident and calm, especially in the adrenaline filled jittery moments just before the big event.

Warriors keep their fear under control by going over the script again and again, like a checklist.

Remember to always create a script – called a *game plan* among athletes – embody it, review it, and rehearse it repeatedly before any big event.

Framing: Framing is a technique used to shape how you think and feel about a situation.

You can use framing to make hugely important events seem run of the mill. For example, you can reduce performance anxiety by re-framing an *exam* by calling it a *quiz,* or instead of saying "I'm going for a *run,*" say, "I'm going for a *jog.*"

Warriors commonly frame battles using three explanatory styles:

- "This is just like another day of training."
- "This is business, and I have a job to do."
- "*Whatever* happens, this will be a valuable learning experience."

You can use this three-pronged approach to frame anything you have worked hard to prepare for and avoid psyching yourself out when it comes time to perform.

By re-framing big challenges to make them seem commonplace, you can mitigate fear.

Othering: Warriors create powerful alter-egos or *Virtual Selves* using a method called *Othering*.

Othering requires creative thinking and the use of your imagination. The goal is to create a self-fulfilling prophecy by transforming your reality into what you fantasize it to be.

Warriors use imagery to create a parallel universe that we step into once we have embodied the character or avatar. Right before I go into battle, I go ahead and do my pre-battle ritual. Those who know me know that I have a gorilla tattooed on my right forearm. The gorilla is also in the logo for the Afrikan Martial Arts Institute. So, during my ritual, I awaken the inner gorilla...I rock back and forth and I have visions of a gorilla charging across an open field. He pounds his chest powerfully just as lightning strikes and thunder booms. I hear the thunder and see the lightning hit the ground as I roar. You hear me roar and you look at my eyes and you know I am ready to go to war.

An old friend in my Special Forces unit once told me that he manages not to worry about going into battle because he pretends it's a video game. He said: "I pretty much think of all our missions as a video game. I have a little energy bar and a stamina bar above my head and every time I get hit, that bar goes down, but every second that I don't get hit that goddamned bar goes back up and even gets longer, until I'm damn near invincible."

You can use your imagination to create an invincible character the next time that you find yourself in a competitive situation. Use role models to form this character and role-play, pretending you *are* this person. Make yourself a "legend in your own mind" and then embody the part like an actor would. You can become anyone you imagine.

CHAPTER FIVE
CRIME PREVENTION

There are a lot of situations that we are not equipped to face alone. We need someone's help, but that someone does not have to be and, if you're of Afrikan descent, should *not* be, the police! So call a friend instead of the cops!

We have long been brutalized by the police throughout America and, indeed, the world. *Officer Friendly* is more like *Stranger Danger*. And a large part of our training should be defense against sticks, knives and guns – the tools of the brutal bastards in blue's trade.

What is the function of police; what do they do?

They certainly do not *prevent* crime; they arrive after the damage is done.

But the *prevention* of crime is our greatest concern when dealing with criminals.

And what, exactly is a crime?

A crime is an act prohibited by the state – or an omission of an act mandated *by* the state – wherein this act, or omission, is subject to punishment by the state after the offender is arrested by the police, prosecuted by a public prosecutor, and convicted after a court proceeding by a judge with or without a jury. All crimes are, by definition, crimes against the state, so the abolishment of crime is simple: abolish crime by abolishing the state.

When we talk about crime in this book, we are referring to violent and non-violent actions that cause some form of loss – loss of health; loss of property; loss of freedom; loss of sanity; loss of humanity; loss of life.

Below are effective ways to prevent crime:

Situational Awareness

The first step in crime prevention is to develop an awareness and presence of mind to spot potential dangers in advance and take steps to avoid them. Naturally, the degree of alertness you should employ depends on your environment. At home, the workplace and friends' homes you can, of course, drop your guard a bit, however, when traveling or when out in public, your guard should be up.

When you are out in strange surroundings, stay alert, walk with a purpose, and be attentive to your surroundings. If you feel suspicious of the area or people around you, prepare yourself mentally for an attack. Have a plan of action you follow if you are attacked and be ready to execute that plan. Consider where you could run to escape if need be, such as the nearest retail shop or restaurant.

When you enter a public area, do a quick scan of your surroundings for possible trouble. Make a mental note of anyone too loud and obnoxious, the drunks, and the brooding loners. Note exits and cul-de-sacs, and always sit facing the entrance.

Posture

A major deterrent to crime is *posture*.

Your posture is part of your body langauge. Good posture and a strong, fluid walk communicate to people around you a sense of confidence and strength.

Criminals often target victims that appear weak and easy to intimidate. Consciously or instinctively, they tend to choose people whose body langauge communicates a weak and vulnerable disposition. Good posture sends out signals that indicate strength, confidence, and awareness, thereby helping to prevent an attack. Most criminals would think twice about attacking someone with such a confident posture and would simply wait for a more suitable victim to come by.

Safe Distance

Safe Distance is the minimum distance you should maintain between you and a suspicious person or car. This distance is between four to eight feet from you. The reason for keeping safe distance is that there is a time lapse in the nervous system between perception and reaction – approximately 0.5 seconds.

This means that if a stranger can come closer than Safe Distance, then that stranger could "steal on you." To get "stole on" means you have been "sucker punched" or "blindsided" – you have fallen victim to a sudden unprovoked attack before you had time to react. However, maintaining safe distance forces a potential attacker to take two steps towards you first before he can hit you. This gives an alert person enough time to evade and escape or counter-attack.

If a potential attacker moves in close, tell him or her to keep their distance. Do not be embarrassed to shout at people to back away if you feel threatened or uncomfortable. If they continue to move closer, back away to maintain the Safe Distance while demanding they back off. Any further advances towards you should then be interpreted as an attack and you should react accordingly.

Crime Prevention Strategy

Most crimes follow a four-stage progression:

- *Opportunity*
- *Interview*
- *Positioning*
- *Attack*

Before a predator can attack, he or she needs an *Opportunity* – a potential victim or target at a time and location that is advantageous to the criminal.

The *Interview* is the stage in which the predator tries to gauge the level of resistance or compliance the potential victim may offer, or the security measures in place around a potential target.

An assertive response at this stage, or the display of a strong defense, will often result in the predator breaking off from the intended target to search for one more compliant or vulnerable.

The *Positioning* stage is just that, finding the best position from which to launch an attack designed to overwhelm the victim. If a predator has been successful in the previous three stages, he or she will now make the physical *Attack*.

A predator may still call off the attack, however, if the victim is able to create enough commotion and put up a stiff resistance.

Interrupting or stopping the predator at any of the stages can prevent an attack.

The following crime prevention techniques use counter measures to prevent opportunity, avoid the interview, escape the position, and counter the attack:

Home Safety & Defense

The first step to denying criminals an opportunity at your home is to prepare some security measures.

Doors and Windows: Doors and windows provide a false sense of security, since most can be broken using a good kick. Without the threat of a response, glass windows and sliding doors offer no defense against intruders. In time of civil disorder, natural disasters, or power blackouts, your home will be vulnerable.

The first defense, then, is to improve the integrity of the home. Foremost is to have solid core, hardwood or metal doors on all exterior entrances, complete with heavy-duty doorframes and dead-bolt locks. Even a solid door can be easily opened with a crowbar unless the doorframe is solid as well.

Make sure all potential entrances are secure, including neighboring structures such as garages, which are a favorite target for burglars particularly if they have a door connecting the garage to the house.

Even if you have a CCTV (*Closed Circuit Television*) camera at the entrance, also install a fisheye lens peephole so that during a power blackout you can still check who is at the door without opening it.

Windows may need burglar bars or grates to prevent entry, but one danger is that they can prevent escape in case of a fire. Consult with local fire safety standards before you install burglar bars. Burglar bars installed on exit doors or windows of sleeping rooms should be equipped with a quick release device that allows them to be opened from the inside without the use of a key, separate tool or any special knowledge or effort.

Equip all entrances and garages with motion sensor lights and if possible, have an extra switch for all exterior lights in the master bedroom.

If you have the sliding patio-style doors, install a patio door bar – commonly called a *Charley Bar*. These doors are easy to jimmy and usually have poor quality locks. Many can also be simply lifted up off their rails and removed.

Leave on a light and a radio or television when you leave the house. Before breaking into a house a burglar will stop and listen for sounds of occupation, the noise from the TV or radio may act as a deterrent. Draw the curtains or blinds at night.

Should you return home and discover signs of entry, do not enter the house or call out. Whoever entered your home may still be there, busy either stealing or perhaps waiting for you to return home. Instead, go to a neighbor or public area and phone your comrades for assistance.

Keys and Locks*:* Change all the locks on exterior doors when you move into a new house or apartment. Previous tenants, their friends, and neighbors may all have keys to your front door.

Do not leave spare house keys under the doormat or in the planter. Burglars routinely check these places.

In many apartment complexes, property management keeps a copy of the key to your apartment. The reason is in case of an emergency, or for maintenance purposes, they may need to access your apartment even if you are not home. The danger is that you never know who has access to these keys. Anyone with access can enter your apartment at any time. While living in Arizona, I was the head of security for a chain of apartment complexes. In one complex, people's homes were being stolen from with no sign of forced entry. It turned out that the complex's maintenance supervisor was using the spare keys to enter tenants' apartments when they weren't home and steal jewelry and electronics. He had even set up hidden camera in several women's bedrooms and bathrooms. Property management companies seldom do background checks, so a recently hired convicted rapist could just walk into the office and steal or make a copy of your door key that he can use days or years later to enter your home.

To protect yourself, ask to see where the keys are stored and what security measures are in place to prevent unwanted access. For example, are they stored in a safe or locked cabinet where only the senior manager has a key, or are they hung on pegs in the open or in an unlocked closet.

If the property management company requires a copy of your house key it is usually written into the rental agreement and so if you change your lock without providing a copy key to the management office you will be in violation.

However, if you think security is inadequate to protect you and your family, then ignore the rental agreement and change the locks. Your safety outweighs a rental agreement.

At the very least have another strong lock installed that can only be locked from the inside and does not require an outside key. This way you can ensure that while you are at home no one can silently enter with the front door key.

Apartments: In high-rise apartment buildings, remember to lock the balcony doors and install a *Charley Bar* even if you do not live on the ground floor, since it may be possible to climb from one balcony to another.

Get to know the other people on your floor so that you have someone to run to in case of emergency.

Never remain alone in an apartment laundry room, mailroom, or parking garage.

Do NOT enter an elevator if you are suspicious of the occupants, wait for the next one. When you are on an elevator, stand close to the door; if you do not like the looks of the person getting on, you can quickly dash out before the doors close.

If you are attacked in an elevator, push all the floor buttons. This means the elevator will stop at every floor giving you a greater chance of escaping or calling for help. Do NOT push the emergency stop button. This will stop the elevator between floors with you and your assailant. Most tenants are so accustomed to false alarms they are not likely to be concerned by the elevator alarm sounding again.

Strange Noises: To become accustomed to the strange noises that you hear at night after moving into a new house or apartment, do the following exercise:

1. Turn on all the lights and, with a friend if necessary, make sure the house is empty by checking every room and closet.

2. Lie down in your bedroom with your eyes closed and listen to the various sounds around you. Try to identify unusual or strange noises by tracking the source. In this way, you will be able to recognize suspicious noises from the everyday sounds made by the building. Then if you are awakened in the night by a strange noise of an intruder, you will not confuse it for the everyday sounds made by the building and vice versa.

Strangers: Should a stranger come to your door asking to use the phone because of an emergency, offer to make the call yourself, but do not allow that person to enter your home.

A common ploy is for a disheveled and bleeding "accident victim" to beg for assistance. This tactic has even been employed in movies and television shows and it never works out well for anyone who lets the victim inside the house. Once the door is open, the "victim," or his accomplices, rush in afterward.

If the person is truly injured, he or she will be just as safe sitting on your doorstep while you phone for help.

Delivery/Repairperson: Request identification from all delivery and repair persons.

Phone the company to verify their description. If you feel there is something suspicious, then look up the number in the public directory rather than the number that may appear on the I.D. or invoice since there may be accomplices answering the phone.

A few years ago, I was at the new home of a priest. While the priest was upstairs getting changed so we could go work out, a Caucasian man showed up to "turn on the gas." He asked me to handle it, so I went to the door, cracked it open – as they had no peephole – and asked for the man's identification. The man scowled and said "Look, man, I have on a company uniform, what more identification do I need?"

"Look, *boy*," I said, knowing he would never be allowed in the house now. My hand crept toward the knife in my pocket "Show your identification!"

The man's fist balled up. I deployed my knife behind the door. Suddenly, a Black man pulls up in a gas company truck and shouts "Oh, I thought I had this job."

The Caucasian man turns and walks down the stairs, shouting "You can take it! This guy's crazy!"

He left...in a non-company pickup truck.

I told the priest what transpired. That same day, he got a new door with a peephole installed.

Valuable items that could be pocketed should be removed from the working area before the repairperson arrives. Lead him directly to the area that is in need of repair. Do not allow him or her to wander about the house or follow you around. Be friendly, but leave the repairperson alone to do the work.

Do not talk about intimate and familiar subjects. If he or she makes obvious sexual overtures, then say that your significant other will be home shortly. If he or she continues to make advances, threaten to call his or her company and lodge a complaint. If the person is still not discouraged, slip away and phone your comrades for help or deploy that weapon you SHOULD have on you anytime a stranger is allowed inside your house.

Statistics show 65.8 percent of burglaries occur at residences. Most residential burglaries – 62.0 percent – occur during the daytime. Also, 50% of rapes occur within the victim's home.

Obscene Phone Calls: There are certain individuals, usually men, who derive excitement and pleasure from harassing innocent victims through the telephone. Most are smart enough to use prepaid phone cards, so even though the phone company keeps a record of all calls on your phone, they may still not be able to identify the caller.

Most obscene phone calls are not a prelude to actual attacks and are just annoying. However, if threats of violence are made towards you, your loved ones, or your property, this is a serious offense that should not be taken lightly.

Never admit on the phone, or at the door, that you are alone. Hang up the instant you realize it is an obscene call. Do not yell, scream, blow a whistle, or engage in any conversation with the caller, as this is likely to encourage him. A non-reaction will discourage callers that enjoy hearing fear or disgust in their victims.

If calls continue, keep a written record of the date, time, and what was said. Notify your Phone Company and your comrades. Get call identification, call blocking, or use the *69 button function to trace the last call. Contact your phone company for more information about these services. Do not attempt to call the offender.

The Safe Room

Ancient castles in the Oyo Empire, in Nigeria, had a *redoubt* – a place of last refuge in which the Alaafin ("Emperor") could retreat if the palace was under siege and await reinforcements. In an apartment or house, you can also build a redoubt or *safe room* to retreat to if intruders enter the home while you and/or your loved ones are there.

In addition to defense against intruders, having a Safe Room can also be a lifesaver in the event of a natural or manmade disaster. A safe room is also a critical requirement for women and families who are being stalked.

The best location to designate a safe room is in or near the master bedroom, since the most likely time you would be surprised by an intruder is when you are sleeping. A bedroom with a connecting bathroom is best. Be sure to instruct other members of the family, especially children, that if any emergency occurs when they are home alone, they should run to the safe room, lock the door, call you and wait until you or your emergency team of comrades arrive. This will give you some peace of mind knowing that, in the event of a serious situation, the children have a plan to find relative safety.

Construction: A safe room should be equipped with a strong exterior-type door. Most interior doors are useless for preventing entry, since they are lightly constructed and can be easily kicked in. Buy a solid wood or steel composite door, normally used as an exterior door, and have it installed in place of your regular interior door. A door is only as strong as its frame so you will probably have to reinforce your existing doorframe as well. Finally, install two strong bolt locks that can only be locked from the inside. Do not bother with door chains and other locks that allow you to open the door only a couple of inches, as they are useless. Instead, use floor bars and foot locks. The stronger you can make the entrance to your safe room, the better.

If the safe room has external windows that can be accessed from the ground or an adjoining structure, you should reinforce them as well. Also, install heavy curtains to ensure that no one from the outside can see what is happening in your safe room or can tell how many people are inside by watching the shadows on the curtains.

Equipment: The room should have a telephone. A cell phone AND a landline is best, but if you only have one option, choose a cell phone, as intruders will cut your landline. Be sure to keep that phone fully charged at all times.

A Short Wave or Citizen Band ("CB") radio is also a must have and is especially handy if cell phone services are disrupted.

Store one or more weapons to use as a last line of defense should an intruder succeed in breaking into the safe room. A 12-gauge shotgun, using buckshot, is excellent for home defense. For smaller framed people and children, a 20-gauge shotgun works well. Do NOT use slugs in the shotgun, pistols, or rifles as rounds can penetrate walls and doors and hit family members or neighbors. You should also have a few extra knives handy.

Your safe room should also be equipped with several bottles of water, several energy bars and a first aid kit, in the event of a natural disaster or emergency.

Finally, if you have surveillance equipment installed as part of a home alarm system, make sure you have a monitor installed in your safe room so that you can monitor what is going on in and outside your property from the safety of your safe room.

Defense Against Home Intrusion

If strange noises come from outside of the house, and, if it is possible to reach the light switches without being spotted, turn on the outside lights, grab your home protection weapons and observe from a place of cover and concealment.

If you are awake when an intruder breaks in through the front door, quietly run out the back door. Do not allow yourself to be trapped inside your home alone where there is little likelihood of anyone coming to your aid. Screams coming from your house, even if heard by neighbors, are likely to be shrugged off as coming from the television or a domestic dispute.

If you hear noises coming from inside the house, do not immediately turn on the interior lights. The intruder is in unknown territory while you are in your own element; the darkness works to your advantage. Stay hidden, lock the bedroom door or retreat to a safe room. If you have a weapon in the bedroom, get it.

If you are alone and you hear movement in the house do NOT call out, as some so-called "experts" suggest. Doing so gives up your position. Do not EVER assume the intruder is simply some idiot seeking to steal your costume jewelry and will run when you shout "Aisha, grab the shotgun, I heard a strange noise!" or "I warn you...I'm armed." Do that and the NEXT strange noise you hear just might be the sound of bullets fired in YOUR direction.

The smarter option is to stay hidden, quiet and ready to attack, with stealth, from a place of cover and concealment.

If you awake to find an intruder in your bedroom, do NOT pretend to remain asleep as these "experts" also often suggest. Once again, don't assume the intruder is dumb. If he has come to assassinate you, or to rape you, you just aided in your victimization. Leap out of that damned bed and attack with speed and ferocity. Your life – and the life of your loved ones – depends on it.

Bad Neighbors

In survival, the greatest potential threats are usually the ones closest to you. A potential source of danger and misery are your neighbors and chances are that some are either criminals, mentally unstable, or psychopaths. Living next door to these types of people can make your life a living hell and even become life threatening.

Two houses from us lives a single mother who has three sons around 10-13 years old and one who is about 4 years old. They run around, breaking everyone's property, climbing people's trees and sitting on their mailboxes. They came to the house a few times, asking to play with my son, Oluade, who is a teenager and my youngest daughter, Oriyemi, who is younger than all of them except the four year old. I said yes, hoping that my children could teach the boys something positive. They ended up attacking my daughter with sticks because my children aren't Christians. Oluade ran them off.

While I was at home alone, working on the upcoming book, *Jagunjagun: The Afrikan Art of War,* I heard voices on the side of the house. I peered out the window, but did not see anyone, then I heard mumbled voices again in my back yard. I armed myself and peered back there. I did not see anyone, but could hear someone fiddling with the basement door. I positioned myself in the shadows and waited.

A few minutes later, I saw the three older boys at my kitchen door, attempting to force their way into the house by jimmying the lock. I concealed my weapon and charged toward the door. When they saw me, they damned near defecated in their pants. They ran off shouting "Damn, that nigga was home!" and "I didn't even SEE that nigga, until he was right up on us!"

I went to their house and told their mother, who denied it was them, claiming they were playing in their own back yard all day. When I told her I saw them with my own eyes and would handle it MY way if SHE didn't, she faked being angry at them and told them to stay away from our property.

The next day, the oldest boy saw my son and said "Man, yo' daddy was trippin'! We was just gon' take yo' bike and ride it for a li'l bit, then put it back."

No remorse; no caring what harm they would have caused. That boy, and perhaps his brothers, too, is a secondary psychopath, made that way by a psychopathic system.

If you plan to move to a new home, take extra time to check out the neighborhood and try to find out if there are any good reasons to avoid moving in. Ask your realtor if the neighborhood has a tenant/homeowner' s association or community guidelines that tend to prevent bad neighbors from moving in.

Knock on a couple of neighborhood doors and speak with the locals. Introduce yourself and explain that you are thinking of moving into the area and you were wondering if the neighborhood is safe for your children or for women. If there are serious problems with some of the people living in the area, you will soon find it out.

Drive by at night and see if things change after dark. An area may seem quite innocent during the day but can become a madhouse at night.

If you get a bad feeling about the place or neighbors, and you have a choice, then find another place to move. If you have no choice, or if new neighbors move in, and you find yourself being harassed or infringed upon, here are a few actions you can take.

Diplomacy: The first approach is to be diplomatic. Make sure you have an accurate assessment and that you are not overreacting. Talk to other neighbors to find out if they feel as strongly about the problem as you do. Also, ensure that you are not likewise in some contradiction to community ordinance or standard that would undermine your own claims of being the innocent victim.

Write down a list of your complaints and include times and dates. This will help you to be more organized and better able to communicate your concerns if, or when, you approach your neighbor. In addition, if diplomacy fails and you need to take a legal course, you will have a much better case if you have written documentation.

If you feel your complaints are justified, your next step is to communicate with the offending neighbors. If done under the guise of good neighborliness, your initial talk can have a good chance of success. If your approach is angry and accusatory, you are likely to elicit a similar response and make the situation worse.

In a best-case scenario, your neighbor recognizes the problem, apologizes and works to correct it. Some may even react with surprise, not realizing they had been disrespectful or annoying.

In a worst-case scenario, the neighbor reacts with anger and threats. Stay calm and do NOT get into a shouting match. If the animosity increases, your neighbor may end up becoming a vindictive nuisance or even a vengeful stalker.

If nothing improves, the next step is to write your neighbor a detailed and formal letter. Make the tone of your letter businesslike. You can cite sections from your homeowner's association or community guidelines, but do not threaten or talk about legal actions you could take. Keep copies of all letters and complaints you file.

Proactive: If the problem continues or escalates, you will need to step up your defensive strategies. Check with other neighbors to see if you have allies and get them on your side. Chances are that if your troublesome neighbors are bothering you, they are also bothering others.

File a formal complaint with your property owner, property manager, or tenant/homeowner association via a registered or notarized letter. Registered mail is essential for building a legal case if you need to in the future.

Demand that your property owner go and speak to your neighbors and that you be debriefed afterward.

If there is no improvement, send a second registered letter, specify the disruptions and/or violations, and reference your first letter. Mention the obvious ineffectiveness of that previous effort.

Legal: If, by this time, the situation has not improved, you may consider getting the advice of an attorney. Do an internet search of tenant and homeowner law and review your lease. If you rent your property, check with local housing clinics to see if there are any grounds for you to withhold paying rent. Withholding rent will help to motivate the property owner to remedy the situation. Leases are usually written with much attention to details that favor the property owners, but, like any contract, it cannot infringe on any legal statutes or your civil rights. If your neighbors are in any way inhibiting you from enjoying those rights, you have grounds to act.

If they damage your property, consider suing, but only in extreme circumstances. Contact law enforcement if there is damage, and ask for a police log entry to assist with insurance claims.

Finally, as unfair as it sounds, moving out may be your best option. Either that or live in a perpetual state of war.

CHAPTER SIX
TRAVEL SAFETY

The maxim of military strategy 'know your terrain' applies equally well to personal defense. Know where you are going and what the local terrain will be.

Whenever you go on vacation, visit friends, attend a new school, or plan to spend time in unfamiliar areas, find out what the environment is like. Ask locals – waiters, bartenders, taxi drivers, tourist and travel agents, and the like – questions, such as "Is the area known for crime?" "Is there a lot of police activity?" "Do buses and taxis come there after dark?" "Is there an area you should avoid?"

Bad Neighborhoods

There is not a city in the world that does not have an area known for crime and danger. Simply walking or driving through these areas can be dangerous and thus should be avoided if possible. If you are in a strange city and have not had a chance to find out which neighborhoods to avoid, then look for common signs that you may be in a dangerous area. These include:

- Lots of old, beaten-up cars parked on the street or driving around

- Numerous liquor stores, pawn shops, and check cashing outlets in the area

- Businesses and shops that all have heavily barred windows and doors

- A lot of empty lots and abandoned buildings

Also, remember that there are plenty of areas that are relatively safe during the day but become dangerous at night. These include many of the downtown and industrial parts of most cities.

I would also recommend staying away from the party districts in major cities at night – Rush Street, in Chicago; Buckhead, in Atlanta; Bourbon Street, in New Orleans – as Afrikans are treated poorly in these areas and often harassed by police.

If you stray into what you think is a bad area, go back out the way you came, if you can, unless you know that there is a quicker way out ahead.

What To Do If You Get Lost

If you are lost in a bad neighborhood:

- Lock all vehicle doors

- Get out flashlights, phones and maps

- Do not get out of the car

- If you sense immediate danger, drive off and call a comrade. Look for street signs and any identifying points you can tell your comrade

Backtrack: Make a U-turn if you are on a two-way street and go back the way you came. If you cannot make a U-turn, turn right or left at the next intersection, then right or left again to get you headed back to where you came from.

If you are near a freeway, look for an entrance ramp. If there is one, take it – even if it only goes in the opposite direction you were headed. Once on the highway, you can turn back at the nearest safe-looking exit. It is better to take a few extra minutes driving out of your way than to remain in a dangerous situation.

Plot a New Course: If backtracking does not work and you find yourself driving even *deeper* into the bad area, then plot a new course. Find a safe place to stop and look at your map. Pull out your cell phone and call a spouse, friend, relative or comrade to alert them to your situation.

Locate your present position on your map. Mark your map with your present position and look for the nearest freeway on-ramp for the direction you want. Make sure that getting there does not take you through more of the bad neighborhood.

If you cannot find an on-off ramp reasonably close, as a last resort, look on your map for any kind of major street that you can head for. The point is simply to get into a safer part of town.

If you do not have a map, turn on your GPS unit, or use the one on your cell phone. Follow the directions from your GPS back to the freeway or major road you were originally on before you got lost.

Defense Against Carjacking

Continued advances in automobile anti-theft technology have made it increasingly more difficult for thieves to steal cars. As a result, the best way now to steal a car is to carjack one with the driver still inside. In this way, the jacker can take the car keys and thus does not have to find a way to override the car's alarm system. Not surprisingly the incidents of carjacking are increasing and will likely continue to do so.

A carjacking can occur at any location where a car and driver slows down. These include shopping centers, ATMs, parking lots, self-serve car washes, self-serve gas stations, convenience stores, hotels, any fast food drive-thru, and driveways as the driver gets in or out of the car.

There are four common tactics used by carjackers:

Ambush: In an ambush, an assailant will wait out of view and suddenly attack as you are either leaving or entering your vehicle. Assaults in public parking areas are not confined to when you are returning to the car. If there is a place where an attacker can lurk undetected, he may choose to make a surprise attack just as you are opening your door.

Defenses Against the Ambush:

- Become more aware whenever you are parking or going to your automobile. Be aware of any people within a 30-foot radius around you when you are walking to and from your vehicle.

- Always look for the parking spot that has the most potential for safety. In a large garage with elevators, this means parking as close to an elevator as you can. If that is not possible, go for the next closest from an elevator that still has good illumination.

  In an open parking lot, park as close to the mall entrance as possible yet away from structures that could afford a hiding place to a potential attacker. Also, park as close or under a streetlight even in the daytime. If you return after nightfall, you can better see your car and check the area around your car. Remember that many parking areas can be busy and full of people during office hours but can become deserted after hours and ripe for carjackers, rapists, and robbers.

  Do not leave any packages or luggage in the car, even if they contain nothing valuable, thieves do not know this and will break into your car causing damage and inconvenience for nothing.

- In multi-story parking garages you should avoid using stairs because they are often dark and little used. However, there may be circumstances where stairs are safer than an elevator, but that is a judgment call only you can make at the time.

- Keep your pepper spray or other self-defense tool in hand when exiting or returning to your vehicle. Also, have your keys in your hand when approaching your car so that you do not have to linger before entering your vehicle.

- If you are returning to your car and you see someone or something suspicious in your path or near your car, go no farther. Return to where you came from and call a friend or comrade to come accompany you to your vehicle. If no one is nearby, prepare to deploy your weapon and observe your car and the suspicious person or activity around it from a position of cover and concealment.

- If your car has a remote door opener, it probably also has a panic button. This button is usually red or has a special texture. Pushing this button will turn on your car's alarm. If you see a suspicious person or persons lurking near your car, you can use the panic button to activate the alarm from a distance to scare off any potential attackers without revealing your location. In addition, if you are surprised by an attacker as you are approaching your car you can activate the alarm to try to attract attention and assistance.

- When you get back in your car, lock your doors immediately. If you are buckling your baby in the car seat, put the baby in the car seat and buckle him/her up quickly. Do not become preoccupied, thus vulnerable, with arranging hats, bibs, pacifiers, and the like. This can wait until you are in your seat with the doors locked.

- If you are outside your car when *attacked*, try to keep the car between you and the assailant, crawl under the car if necessary. If the attacker is armed and you are not, or he or she gets the drop on you, and they want your vehicle, give it to them. Do not get into a possibly lethal situation over something you can always replace later.

  However, if the carjacker wants to take you hostage, or is intent on hurting you, fight for your life.

- If you must get into a car with the assailant, try to keep your hand on the door handle and make sure the door is unlocked. Be prepared to jump out just as the car begins to accelerate, or when it stops at a busy intersection.

If the assailant is driving, wait until he stops at an intersection. If you can, grab the keys and escape. If you cannot escape, then try to take the keys and throw them out the window.

If you are carjacked and forced to drive, run red lights honking your horn to attract attention, drive to a busy gas station and park, unevenly, near the station's store.

If you are forced into the trunk of your car, feel around for the emergency trunk release. This is a 'T' shaped handle attached to a short cord that will release the trunk when pulled. Open the lid slightly to see out. As soon as the car comes to a stop in an area that is well lit and you can see a safe area to run to, escape. Be aware that an accomplice may be following your stolen vehicle in another vehicle, so run as quickly as possible, but do NOT run to another person's car for help. If it appears that you are being driven into the wilderness you may have to jump out even if the car is still moving.

If your car does not have an internal trunk release, feel around for anything that can be used as a weapon – a crowbar, a jack, a flashlight, an umbrella; anything and then get ready to fight for your life when that trunk opens.

Bump and Jack*:* In this scenario, the carjacker rear-ends your car. When you get out of the car to inspect the damage and exchange license and insurance information, the carjacker jumps in your car and drives away or produces a weapon and makes you give up the car; an accomplice drives the carjacker's car away at the same time.

Defense Against the Bump and Jack:

- If another driver bumps you in traffic, stay alert. Roll up your windows and lock your doors. The type of damage that would occur during a bump and jack is deliberately kept to a minimum so that the victim is less likely to call the police on the cell phone right away.

- Look at the driver and passengers of the other vehicle before getting out of your car to exchange info. Are they young men? Are there other cars close by? If the situation makes you apprehensive, write down in your notebook, or text to yourself, the vehicle's license plate number and its description – color, make and model.

- Signal to the other driver to follow you and drive to a police station or a populated, well-lit area. If you get out of your car, continue to be suspicious and make sure you take your keys and purse/wallet with you.

- If the other driver wants you to roll down your window when you signal him to follow, do NOT. Simply write, "Follow me to police station" in your notebook and hold it up so he can read it through the window. If it is an honest accident then the other driver should have no reluctance to follow you and make a report.

The Pullover: The carjackers pulls up next to you and signals you that you have a mechanical problem, or a flat tire. Carjackers have even been known to follow a target vehicle while a passenger throws stones onto the back bumper to make it sound as if there is a real problem before they pull up to signal the driver. When you pull over to investigate, they draw weapons and steal your car.

On city streets, it may be someone on the sidewalk that signals you or asks for directions with the same intention. On less trafficked roads, the carjacker may pretend to have a breakdown or accident and attempt to flag a potential victim down under the pretense of requiring assistance.

Defense Against the Pullover:

- If someone is signaling you to pull over, slow down, turn off the radio if it is playing, and then listen and feel for anything unusual in either the sound of the engine or in the handling of the vehicle. If you *do* have a flat tire, you can feel this through the steering wheel and you will notice a tendency to drift, either to the left or right, depending on which side of the car the flat tire is on.

- If you *do* hear or feel something unusual with the vehicle, slow down, turn on your hazard lights and continue to drive until you come to either a busy, well lit area or a gas station. Remember, you can continue to drive even with a flat tire provided you remain under 25 miles per hour.

- Do NOT stop to offer help to a stranded motorist. Instead, roll down the widow and offer to stop at the next telephone and call for help, or call roadside assistance – 4-1-1 – from your cell phone.

- If you *do* pull over to investigate or lend assistance at a traffic accident, stop behind the other cars. At night, keep the headlights directed onto the scene, leave the motor running, and do NOT get out unless you are reasonably sure there are no signs of danger. Scan nearby vegetation for anyone hiding in the bushes. If the road is flanked by a gully or ditch, check for anyone lying down in it.

- If you suspect someone is following you, drive to the nearest gas station, drive-through restaurant, or busy intersection and blow the horn.

- If you are a single woman, or a woman who is often driving alone in a vehicle, keep a man's style hat or cap in the car. Wear it if you are waiting for mechanical assistance or if you are driving alone at night. By wearing the hat, your silhouette will appear to be that of a man's, which will deter anyone looking for women to victimize.

The Box: Carjackers stop at a red light or stop sign in front of your vehicle. The carjackers quickly jump out of their car and run up to your window and produce a weapon to force you out of the car. An accomplice remains in the vehicle and they all drive away together. More professional carjackers may have a second vehicle pull up behind so that you cannot back up, completely boxing you in.

Another variation is to have a pedestrian at either a crosswalk or while you are stopped at a red light walk in front of your car to delay and distract you while an accomplice runs up to your window from behind a parked car or other cover. The accomplice will either pull you from your vehicle or produce a weapon to rob you of it.

Defense Against the Box:

- Make it a habit that whenever you come to a stop behind another vehicle, you always leave enough space between you and the car in front of you so that you can see their rear wheels. This will give you enough room to sharply turn and go around the lead car, either along the shoulder or over the sidewalk, if necessary, to escape.

- If someone is standing in front of the car to prevent you from driving away, continue driving forward slowly, gradually increasing speed. If that person refuses to move, well...

- If an attacker reaches in through the window, grab his wrist, quickly roll up the window and trap his arm, injure the arm in whatever way possible and then speed off with his arm trapped. I witnessed this done to a carjacker many years ago, when I was a young man. The jacker tried to pull a woman out of her car. Before I could make it to the car to assist her, she had pulled his arm to her chest and then sped off. You could hear the jacker's screams a block away as his arm was dislocated and fractured, as were both his ankles as she drug him up the street.

- Your safety must trump the well-being of the car AND the carjackers. If you are being boxed in by other cars, and it is obvious they mean you harm, you have to be willing to let them know you will stop at nothing to escape by running your car into the other cars...and into the jackers.

Car Breakdowns

Keep your vehicle in good shape and keep a "Get Home Bag" in the trunk. Never allow your gas tank to drop below half a tank.

Everyone old enough to drive a car should learn some basic car repair. Know how to connect the battery, jump-start a dead battery, check the oil and radiator fluid, and change a tire. These simple procedures might get you back on the road again.

Even with a flat tire, you can safely drive without ruining the rim provided you drive five miles per hour or less and you drive along the shoulder of the road with your hazard lights on.

Changing a tire at the side of the road is one of the most dangerous activities you can undertake. If you plan to change the tire yourself, ensure that you are safe from oncoming traffic by moving the car as far off the road as you can.

If your car breaks down on a public road, turn on your hazard lights or, if the battery is not functioning, raise the hood and tie a handkerchief or piece of cloth to the radio antenna or door handle nearest passing traffic. Lock the doors and then phone for help. If a stranger offers to help, do not get out of the car; ask the person to phone for assistance if you cannot do so yourself.

If you have car trouble in dark or deserted areas, then turn on your hazard lights or raise the hood of your car, call for assistance and then take out your *get home bag* and find an area off-road and out of sight of passing motorists where you can safely watch your car and wait for help to arrive. If you do not have a phone and you see a place within walking distance that would have a phone, then go there and call for help.

The reason for hiding off the road is that it is becoming more common for criminals to cruise the roads looking for stranded motorists, especially in isolated areas. If they see no one in the car, they may try to rob or vandalize the car but you will be safe from harm as you hide nearby.

Car Breakdowns In The Wilderness

If you have a breakdown in a remote wilderness area, the following survival tips may come in handy.

If in dire need, cannibalize your vehicle for makeshift survival tools:

- A hubcap or sun visor can be used as a snow shovel

- Seat covers and even the foam seat padding can be used as blankets and as added insulation in your jacket or use the foam to fashion footwear to prevent frostbite

- Floor mats can be used as shelter to shut out the wind and rain.

- The car's wiring can be used, like rope, to construct shelters in conjunction with the foam, the floor mats and items from your *get home bag*

To signal for help

- A car horn can be heard up to a mile away. Three long blasts, 10 seconds apart, every 30 minutes, is the *universal distress signal.*

- Burning engine oil in a hubcap provides a black smoke signal that can be seen for miles

- A rear-view mirror can be removed to serve as a signaling device

- Burn a spare tire for signal and/or warmth. Release the air pressure first and use gasoline or oil to ignite it

Get Home Bag

An emergency can strike at any time. Keeping some equipment and supplies in your car ensures that you will always have the necessary survival tools with you wherever you travel. The following are some recommended contents for your bag.

- Flashlights, at least 2
- Self-defense tools, such as pepper spray, a stun gun, and/or a small frame pistol or revolver.
- Batteries for the flashlight
- First aid kit
- Pocketknife

- 2 plastic bottles of water or a filled aluminum water bottle
- 3 protein bars
- Blankets or a sleeping bag
- Mittens, socks and a wool cap
- Extra pair of walking shoes
- Waterproof covering like a tarp or poncho
- Metal coffee can which can be used to heat water
- Small folding shovel
- Booster battery cables
- Emergency road flares and/or warning reflectors
- Bright colored scarf
- Matches in a waterproof case or medicine bottle
- Cigarette lighter
- Candles – a blanket over your head, body heat and a single candle can prevent freezing

In the trunk of your vehicle, also always keep the following items:

- Tool kit
- Paper towel and toilet tissue
- Spare tire
- Rope, tow chain or a strap
- Extra motor oil
- 8' plastic tube to use as a siphon hose
- Map of the area where you plan to travel
- Small book to keep the mind occupied

- Small hand-held CB radio and it's batteries: channel 9 is the emergency channel
- Pen or pencil and paper
- Toiletry kit, soap, washcloth, toothpaste and toothbrush

If there are any warnings of either impending natural disasters or threats of social disasters, you should add to your car kit a small container of fuel and extra engine oil coolant.

In case you are away from home when disaster strikes, or if you have to search for family members, these supplies can extend your range when gas stations are inevitably closed and/or looted.

Car Accidents

If you are involved in a legitimate accident in a populous area of the city, leave your car as close as possible to the place of impact without obstructing traffic. If it is a minor accident, pull all the vehicles involved off the road to avoid obstructing traffic or causing another, more serious, accident.

Securing the Scene: Make sure there are no other hazards or potential accidents. Raise the hood of your car and use your car's hazard warning lights. Set out flares, warning reflectors, or send someone to warn oncoming traffic to slow down. Put out any fires and get away from fuel spills.

Check if anyone is injured. Give first aid if you are qualified and then call for an ambulance. Look around and note the location of the accident before you call for assistance. Tell the emergency operator the name and number of the street and nearest intersection if you know it.

Legal Considerations: In *this* instance, call the police, especially if someone has been injured.

Why?

Because a police report of the accident will help your insurance claim and any liability claims.

Take notes about the accident, such as the time of day, weather conditions, road conditions, streetlights and length of skid marks.

Also, make a diagram of the accident, noting the location of the vehicles, cross walks, stops signs and traffic signals. If you have a camera, take photos or videos of the scene. Date and sign the notes when you are done. These can be invaluable later if you should find yourself sued or having to sue someone else.

Exchange information with the driver of the other car. You should get the following information:

1.   The other driver's name, address, phone number, driver's license number, name of insurance company and policy number

2.   All passengers' names, addresses and phone numbers

3.   Any witnesses' names, addresses and phone numbers

4.   The Vehicle Owner's (if not the driver) name, address, phone number, insurance company and policy number

When you exchange information with the other driver and give facts to the police, DO NOT admit responsibility for the accident. This means not apologizing, even if you think that you were responsible. It may be that a road hazard, mechanical failure, or the other driver was equally at fault. Do not sign any papers or agree to pay for damages. This would imply that you accept responsibility and that can be used against you if there is litigation.

Conversely, do not downplay any injuries you may have and do not accept any gifts or money since this would imply that you have accepted such as equal compensation for your injuries or damages. Your injuries may be more serious than you know.

What To Do After An Accident

Before you allow a tow truck driver to tow your car, be sure to ask the driver how much it will cost and then tell the driver where to take your car. Get the name, address and telephone number of the driver and the towing company.

Even if there are no obvious injuries, both you and your passengers should see a doctor after an accident. The doctor may recognize injuries, sometimes serious, that are not apparent to you. Do not settle claims from the accident until your doctor has advised you about the extent of your injuries.

Take photos of any damage to your vehicle before you have them repaired.

Call your insurance agent as soon as possible after an accident. Your insurance company may have grounds to deny coverage if you fail to give prompt notice of the accident. Follow up the phone call with a written report, including information you noted about the accident, photos of the car damage, and copies of the police report.

Contact a lawyer if you are considering a lawsuit, or if you expect one to be brought against you. Never sign any legal documents or statements without legal counsel.

Public Transportation

Try to avoid waiting or getting off at isolated bus stops when you are alone. Learn the bus schedule so that you can avoid waiting long periods alone at a stop.

If you are standing alone at a bus stop at night, avoid standing directly underneath the light. Standing directly under a light makes it easy for anyone to see that you are alone. Instead, blend into the shadows, away from the light or next to a pole, so that your silhouette does not stand out. This makes it more difficult to spot you from a distance or from cruising automobiles.

If you are a sister traveling alone on a bus or streetcar, try sitting near other women or near the driver. When using subway trains try to sit in the front car from which the motorman operates the train. Sit in an aisle seat so that someone getting on the bus, streetcar or train later cannot trap you in.

Never hesitate to tell someone "stop bothering me," in a loud voice, when others are around. The chances are that your would-be assailant will be more embarrassed than you will.

If someone continues to bother you on the train do not hesitate to deploy your weapon and use it if you have to.

Finally, if you train regularly with a gun club or martial arts school, never wear distinguishing clothing on public transportation. When I was 19, I made this mistake. Wanting to advertise my newly founded martial arts school, I wore my *Indigenous Martial Arts Academy* t-shirt (yeah, I know, Afrikan Martial Arts Institute is a *much* better name; but hey, I was nineteen years old) as I headed to Columbia College on the Chicago "El Train."

Several people took my number and promised to visit my school. Everything was going well...until "Big Crazy" got on the train. *Big Crazy* isn't the man's actual name, I'm sure, but I call him that because he was *big* – about 6'9" tall and about 400 pounds in weight – mostly muscle – and he was *crazy*...nuttier than squirrel poop.

He stared at me for a moment, reading my shirt and then he sat down...next to me. His massive body forced me against the side of the train.

"What's up, man! You do Karate?" he shouted.

"I study indigenous Afrikan Martial Arts," I replied.

"That's *karate*, man...just from Afrika!" he boomed. "Stop trippin'!"

"Okay," I whispered.

"Man, what would you do if I spit in your face right now?" Big Crazy asked.

I glared at him. "Brother, do NOT spit in my face."

"Man...I'll reach in my pants, pull out some shit and throw it in your face!" he screamed, pushing his body into mine.

"If you do, I am going to beat...your...ASS!" I shouted, grimacing in disgust at the thought of this nut making good on his threat.

Big Crazy busted out laughing. "I like you, dude!" he said, rising and walking toward the doors. As he walked off the train he stared at me, smiled and said "I would throw shit in your face, though."

I have never worn any martial arts clothing on public transportation since that day and I never will. You should not either.

Taxi Drivers

Most western nations require taxi drivers to have background checks in order to be licensed. However, in reality, this is rarely done.

The independence taxi drivers enjoy – especially in this age of Über and Lyft, where anyone with a working vehicle can transport passengers for pay – attracts many types of predators to the profession, from thieves to rapists.

While more common in other countries, crimes by taxi drivers can occur anywhere. The most typical crime is overcharging for the standard fare. This can be prevented by having a map and knowing where you are and where you want to go. Question the driver on which route he plans to take and let him see your map so that he knows you are paying attention. Also, ask him how much this trip would normally cost. This will discourage taking long detours and save you some money. However, if there is a dispute in the fare, then just pay it. Often taxis drivers have friends among the police who would turn any argument against your favor.

Tourists and travelers may become victims of even more serious crimes such as robbery, rape and kidnapping. Taxi drivers have been known to work with robbers and will drive their passengers to an isolated area where their waiting cohorts can rob them of their money and baggage. Single women face another danger of being driven to an abandoned area to be raped or even kidnapped and sold into sex slavery – here in Georgia, the kidnapping and sale of women and girls is all too common.

The following can help prevent you becoming a victim of a taxi driver:

- Phone a reputable taxi service listed in the phonebook or online rather than flag one down on the street. Criminals can pose as a taxi service simply by renting or purchasing a used taxi. With listed services, there is a better chance that its drivers are licensed and at least there is a record of your call that can be traced in case you should disappear.

- When possible, have friends or family see you to your taxi. Have them stand by when the taxi arrives and visibly write down the license plate number. Make sure the driver sees them do this. Also, use a phone's camera to take a picture of both the driver and the license plate. It is within your right to do this and most taxi drivers know why you are doing it and will not object.

  If the driver makes a fuss about being photographed, then call another service. This lets a potential attacker know that there are eyewitnesses and hard evidence against him if anything should happen to you.

A criminal posing as a taxi driver can have his pick of victims, so it is very unlikely that he will attack you after all the precautions you have taken. Easier victims are just minutes away.

- Make sure you let some friend or family member know that you are traveling by taxi, where you are going, and what time you are expected to arrive.

Tell them that you will call them when you arrive. If you don't call to confirm your arrival, the friend should then alert comrades and friends in your area.

This is like leaving a travel plan with park rangers before going on a wilderness hike. If you don't show up at the right time and place they will mount a search and rescue.

- Before getting into the cab, make sure the back doors have door handles. If not, don't get in.

If you believe the driver is going off the regular route, tell him to get back to the main streets. If he refuses then tell him to take you back where you came from. If he again refuses, then wait until the vehicle slows down or stops at a stop light and quickly jump out and run in the opposite direction.

Deploy any weapon you have and find the nearest public area or business, and then phone comrades to report the incident and to come get you.

On Foot

Plan your route and avoid shortcuts through parks, vacant lots, alleyways, or unlit areas. Remember to stay alert and walk with a purpose.

Walk near the curb, away from dark alleys and doorways; face oncoming traffic.

Do not overburden yourself with bulky packages and a bulky purse. Carry only the essentials. However, if you are attacked while loaded down, use the packages to your advantage and throw them at the attacker. It may give you the time to run away or deploy your weapon and strike.

When you plan to walk a fair distance, wear footwear and clothing that are comfortable and can allow you to move quickly. High heeled shoes make a distinctive tapping sound that is immediately recognizable to predators waiting for a potential victim to walk by AND they are hard to run or fight in.

If you jog, try to run in groups or pairs especially if you run during times when there is little public traffic, or in isolated areas.

When traveling through strange neighborhoods, be inconspicuous while blending into the background. Dress like the locals – the more different you look, the easier it is to single you out.

Never display large sums of cash in public or wear highly visible and expensive jewelry or clothes.

Do not stop to give directions to a driver or a pedestrian. Asking for directions is a common trap to delay and distract you. However, if you feel you *must* give directions, always ensure a safe distance between you and the other party in order to avoid being surprised by a sudden attack.

Do not allow strangers to stop you on the street for conversations or stop to give beggars change or to light a cigarette. These are stalling techniques used to set up an attack. If you feel so charitable that you are *compelled* to give a beggar your money, make sure you have some small change in your hand ready. When a beggar approaches, hold out your hand and give him the money without slowing your pace.

If you suspect someone is following you, cross the road and walk back in the opposite direction. If the person is truly following you, they will also have to change direction. In addition, if they are intent on attacking you, it is better to see it coming than to be surprised from behind. Head for the nearest well lit or populated area.

If people are within hearing distance, do not hesitate to turn to the person following you and say in a loud voice, "Stop following me!"

If the area is deserted, go to the nearest house that looks occupied, or business premises, or gas station and call a comrade; do NOT go home. You do not want the suspect to know where you live because most attacks occur in the home, out of public view.

CHAPTER SEVEN
COMMON SENSE SELF DEFENSE

Nothing feels better than knowing you can take care of yourself mentally, financially, and physically. Being able to protect yourself in all situations is a confidence booster as much as it is a reassurance and, in many cases, a life saver.

Knowing that common knowledge is not so common nowadays, part of USPI's mission is to teach and train the following effective methods of defense against very types of dangers:

Defense Against A Drunk

Dealing with an obnoxious or aggressive drunk depends on whether the drunk is a friend or stranger.

If he is a stranger and you are in an eating or drinking establishment, notify the management or door staff and let them handle it.

If the drunk is a friend, then gently, but firmly, maneuver the friend into a cab or onto a couch in the family room.

If all else fails and you find yourself fighting a drunk, there is an advantage and disadvantage.

The *advantage* is that alcohol will interfere with his coordination and balance and this will act in your favor during combat. In addition, drunks have a tendency to pass-out because of the depressive effects the alcohol has on the nervous system. A slap to the face may cause just enough shock that the blood pressure falls rapidly, causing unconsciousness.

The disadvantage is that occasionally, alcohol numbs the senses and the drunk will have little sense of pain. As a result, he may continue fighting long after a sober person has quit because of injuries suffered. If this happens, then the only way to stop him is to cause him serious injury, since submission holds will not work, due to the absence of pain.

Recovery Position

If someone passes out from intoxication do not leave them lying on their back. Many have died from suffocating on their own vomit while unconscious in this position.

Instead, bend one of the drunk's knees and use that knee as a lever to roll the drunk over and then lay him on his or her stomach in what is known as the *Recovery Position.* Should they vomit while unconscious, this position will help keep their airway clear.

Money

Avoid carrying large sums of money or unnecessary credit cards when you travel.

Do not carry all your money in one pocket; spread the money out. If you are robbed or pick-pocketed, they will only get one location's worth of money, leaving you the rest.

Carry your identification and credit cards separately from your spending cash.

If you travel through high-risk areas, carry a decoy wad. This is a cheap wallet that has a small stack of money in it with a real money bill on the outside but play money or paper cut to size on the inside. A wallet may also include phony credit cards – cut out credit card ads from a magazine and glue them to cardboard. The decoy should look valuable. If you are robbed, throw the decoy in one direction and carefully and quickly leave in the opposite direction.

Carry your *real* money and cards in a traveler's waist pouch or shoulder holster style pouch that you wear under your clothes.

Do not leave a purse or briefcase unattended in shopping carts, on store counters, in your car, or next to you on the floor in a bathroom stall.

Defense Against_A_Robber

If confronted by a robber or mugger, cooperate. Listen to what he says. Always answer in the affirmative, in a quiet, calm, voice. Be polite. Acting hostile and indignant will only encourage the robber to use a weapon that may or may not be visible.

While you might feel angry and believe you can overpower the robber, it is nevertheless essential that you pretend to be intimidated. This will allow the robber to relax his guard, then you should launch a swift and vicious surprise attack.

Remember that personal safety is more important than material things. Resist to protect yourself from harm, NOT to protect your belongings.

Try to get a good mental description of the robber; afterwards, jot down some quick notes. Remember any physical characteristics and distinguishing marks such as scars, tattoos, facial hair, hair and eye color, complexion, age, height and weight, and what clothes he was wearing.

If the demand is for money, take out your cash – or your decoy wad – and hold it up for the attacker to see. Then throw it on the ground between you and the assailant while backing away. When he bends to pick up the money, make a run for it. If the assailant is really after only your money, then he will go for the wallet rather than you.

If the robber attempts to move you to another location or restrain you, fight for your life.

Defense Against A Gang

When *I* think of a "gang," I think of Skinheads, Neo-Nazis, the Hell's Angels Motorcycle Club, the Aryan Brotherhood, the KKK and the police. I do NOT think of Crips, Bloods, Vice Lords, Gangster Disciples and 4-Corner Hustlers. These brothers and sisters, with proper guidance and training, would go from being predators of their communities to protectors. This is NOT conjecture, I have witnessed this MANY times. I have friends, family members and comrades who stopped fighting their brothers and sisters after listening to a speech from Dhoruba Bin Wahad, Malcolm X or Minister Farrakhan. I have trained several so-called gangbangers who have gone on to raise families and to become teachers, themselves. MANY of these so-called gangbangers have changed – and nearly ALL of them can...but can the same be said for a Skinhead, Neo-Nazi, or KKK member?

Hell naw!

Put all the teaching and training in the world into a White Supremacist and he is now just an educated – and more dangerous – White Supremacist.

Now that we have cleared that up, let's look at how to handle the REAL gangbangers.

Your first defense is always awareness. Watch for the telltale territorial markers – graffiti. Most gangs mark their turf with graffiti. Caucasian gangs do not usually spray paint their words and symbols on traffic signs and walls, though. They deface their skin. Look for the following tattoos on White Supremacists' hands, arms, faces, necks and sometimes on their vehicles and clothing:

- **The number 14:** Numerical shorthand for the White Supremacist slogan known as the "14 Words," which goes: "We must secure the existence of our people and a future for white children."

- **1488:** A combination of 14, for the "14 Words" above and 88, which stands for "Heil Hitler," as the letter "H" is the 8th letter in the alphabet.

- **Arrow Cross:** Derived from the Hungarian fascist political party known as the *Arrow Cross Party*, active 1935-1945.

- **Blood Drop Cross:** Primary insignia of the Ku Klux Klan. Formally called the MIOAK – *Mystic Insignia of a Klansman.*

- **Boots and Laces:** Skinheads prefer wearing steel-toed work boots, typically with red or white shoelaces.

- **Celtic Cross:** A cross interlocked with, or surrounded by a circle; one of the most common white supremacist symbols.

- **SS Bolts:** A common White Supremacist symbol derived from the Nazi-era symbol for the Schutzstaffel (SS) , whose members ranged from Gestapo agents to Waffen SS soldiers to concentration camp guards.

- **"RAHOWA":** An acronym for **Ra**cial **Ho**ly **Wa**r, a term coined by the *Creativity Movement*, a White Supremacist religion, as a rallying cry for the White Supremacist cause.

If you notice people displaying these symbols, be cautious. They are on the other side of the barricade – your enemy. If you must engage these savages, prepare for battle without quarter.

Look for weapons. Anytime you come across a group of men and women with weapons, whether police, soldiers, militia, or anyone else, exercise extreme caution. Mistakes happen, but when weapons are involved, those mistakes can become fatal.

Another factor that can turn a group violent is alcohol and/or drugs. The effects of alcohol include a relaxing of the brain's inhibitions against impulsive and aggressive behavior. An otherwise normal group of people can turn dangerous when alcohol is involved. Beware of any groups under the influence of drugs or alcohol.

If you happen upon a gang loitering near your route, stop and go back in the direction you came. Be inconspicuous as you quietly escape the area. Better to go out of your way than to present yourself as a potential target.

If it appears a gang has spotted you and is moving towards you, move quickly towards any well-lit and public area where there are more people. If there is a retail shop, café or office building nearby you can duck inside and either wait for the gang to pass by or call for help.

If a gang confronts you, keep your head up but do not stare at anyone, say nothing, do not react, and try not to slow your pace.

If they block your progress, your first line of defense is to use your wits. Speak and reason only with the leader; do not try to win over others to your side. As a rule if you fight one person in the gang, you fight everyone in the gang. So, if you must fight, it is the leader you want to take out first. Make a direct and sudden attack at the leader and do not stop until you see an opportunity to escape. If the gang is only loosely connected, then taking out the leader may put an end to the attack. Drinking buddies feel tough when they are all together, but if the leader, presumably the toughest one among them, falls, then the rest cave in as well. However, in well-established street gangs, like the Skinheads, taking-out the leader will not stop the attack, but it might buy some time to escape as the rest of the gang mentally regroups.

The principle tactic for fighting larger forces is hit and run. If surrounded, quickly attack the weakest point in the circle and try to break through, using injured enemies as barriers between you and the others.

If, while running, you find they are catching up, then stop suddenly, attack the lead pursuer and then run again. Do not let yourself be surrounded, keep moving laterally so that they can only come at you one at a time. While moving, look for a way to summon help or escape.

Use the features in your terrain. Where possible, try to fight in small, narrow, or enclosed spaces. Confined areas negate the advantage of numbers. Stand in the hall or doorway, between parked cars, or between tables in a restaurant. Try to make the terrain between you and the attackers more difficult to cross. Knock things over, such as garbage cans, mailboxes, signs, tables, chairs, and lamps, as you run.

If you are knocked to the ground, lie on your side and use your legs to kick out at the shins and knees of anyone within range. If surrounded on the ground being kicked and beaten, curl up into a ball with the fingers behind your head so the elbows and forearms protect your skull. With the fingers interlaced even if you loose consciousness, the arms will tend to stay in that position offering some protection for your head. Pull your knees into your abdomen and keep your thighs pressed together. As soon as you can spring back to your feet and take off running again.

Sexual Assault

Rape is an act of violence expressed through sex, but is not primarily about sex. Rapists tend to be cowards and therefore victims are most often those that are the most defenseless – children and the disabled or handicapped.

Sexual assault is most commonly committed by a male upon a female although same sex rapes are not uncommon, especially in prisons, military settings, and single-sex schools. Female-on-male rape occurs, but is much less common than male-on-female rape.

Social Situations: Social environments are the hunting grounds for sexual predators. Whenever you go out in public you should be aware of this fact and take precautions.

Use caution in conversations with strangers or within earshot of strangers. Avoid giving your name, address, or place of employment.

When entering any public area, scan the layout for entrances, exits, and any suspicious looking people. This is not only to help you to spot trouble coming, but also in case of fire or earthquake you can escape more quickly.

In bars and restaurants, sit with your back against the wall, preferably with a view of the entrance. Never leave your drink unattended – there are drugs that can be slipped into a drink that can incapacitate your senses and leave you vulnerable to sexual assault.

Remember it is risky to accept a ride home or an invitation for a late night coffee or drink from someone you have just met. This applies to men as well. A common ploy is have an attractive woman meet and pick up traveling businessmen or tourists, then drug and rob them in their hotel rooms. Be careful of whom you are with and where you are when you are drinking alcohol.

Sexual Assault Statistics

- 80 to 90% of rapes are not reported

- 1 in 3 women in the U.S. will be sexually assaulted at some point during their lifetimes

- The typical rape victim is a 16 to 24 year-old woman. However, anyone of either sex, from infants to seniors, can be the victim of rape

- The typical assailant is a 25 to 44 year-old man, who usually chooses a victim of the same race

- Nearly half the time, the victim knows the rapist at least casually, by working or living near him.

- Alcohol is involved in more than 1 out of 3 rapes

- Most rapists plan their attacks, rather than acting on impulse

- Contrary to the admonishment against walking down dark alleys, over 60% of rapes occur in the victim's home. The rapist gains entry by either breaking into the victim's home, or under false pretenses – posing as a repairperson, salesperson or asking to use the phone.

Kidnapping

A kidnapping occurs when a criminal – through fraud, force or threat – moves a person, against his or her will, to another location as part of another criminal activity such as holding the person for ransom, or to sexually abuse the captive. There are three types of kidnappers:

1. Family members who take an offspring
2. Sexual predators
3. Ransom seekers

If a family member has kidnapped your child, the best course of action is to immediately notify comrades and consult an attorney. The second two types are known as *stranger abductions*. The most likely victims of stranger abductions are children and lone women.

Kidnapping can occur as a *crime of opportunity*. In the course of a carjacking, mugging, or home invasion, the assailant(s) may try to move you to another location. To help prevent such initial crimes, follow the previous advice for home invasion, street safety, and carjacking. It is when an assailant tries to transport you that you must make the decision on whether to fight or cooperate.

When To Fight*:* As a rule, fight viciously for your life anytime an assailant tries to take you to another location because the criminal will have a greater advantage, and you will have little chance of escape or rescue, if you go with him or her.

Fight as soon as it becomes obvious that the assailant intends to move you and before the odds are any more in his or her favor.

Most abduction attacks in the U.S. and other "developed countries," are sexually motivated and usually, the intended victim is a woman or child. If you are a woman being abducted, your best chance is to fight back right away.

Escape and Evade: If given the opportunity, RUN. Try to get a good lead on your assailant and run towards well-lit and crowded areas. If the kidnapper is still following you, make the terrain between you and the attacker more difficult to cross. Knock things over as you run.

If you are cornered fight with every ounce of your being. At a minimum, incapacitate him, so he cannot continue to pursue you.

Attract Attention: Scream, yell, run into bystanders, blow a whistle, and bring as much attention as possible to yourself and your attacker. Scream "FIRE!" at the top of your lungs to attract passersby.

Attracting attention works best in or near public places, where the attacker hopes to remain inconspicuous, lest others intervene or call police. You can also attract attention by throwing something heavy through the window of a house if in a residential area, or a storefront in a commercial area. The sound of breaking glass is distinct and always rouses interest. In addition, breaking a store window will set off the alarm, which will attract attention. Better to pay for a broken window than to risk being injured or killed.

If you have escaped the attacker, run to a nearby house or business, let them know what happened and have them call your comrades; they will probably insist on calling the police, too. Don't fight it in this instance. This will help ensure that you are in a safe place, that help is arriving, and that you have witnesses.

Stalkers

There are three basic types of stalkers:

1. Delusional Stalkers
2. Vengeful Stalkers
3. Intimate Stalkers

Delusional Stalkers: These are easy to spot nuts who suffer from a major mental disorder such as schizophrenia, manic depression or erotomania.

They usually have had little if any contact with their victim but due to the peculiarities of their illness, they believe that they have some sublime connection to their victims.

In the cases of erotomania, the stalker may actually be convinced that their victim loves him or her and that they have a relationship, even if they have never met. In another variation, the stalker knows that he and the victim do not presently have a relationship, but that God and/or destiny has deemed that they should be together and the stalker is merely carrying out God's will by stalking the victim.

Delusional stalkers are seldom psychopaths, although they are no less dangerous. Typically, they are unmarried and socially immature loners, who are unable to establish or sustain close relationships with others. They rarely date and have had few, if any, sexual relationships. Since they are both threatened by, and yearn for, closeness, they often pick victims who are unattainable in some way, such as someone already married, or someone in the public eye, like a sports or entertainment celebrity.

Delusional stalkers often come from emotionally abusive or barren backgrounds, and seek to support their fragile identity by having someone from a higher status, such as celebrities and successful professionals, love them.

These types of stalkers often target social and health care professionals, such as therapists, clergymen, doctors or teachers. The understanding and kindness shown to all patients and clients by these professions is blown out of proportion in the mind of the delusional stalker and they interpret professional courtesy shown them as a sign of an intimate relationship.

The Vengeful Stalker: The vengeful stalker is someone that becomes angry with his or her victim over some real or imagined insult. They are mostly low-level psychopaths whose grandiosity and paranoia causes them to interpret everyone's actions as a confirmation of, or direct threat to, their identity.

These stalkers range from the sociopath, who will break a bottle over someone's head that "looked at him wrong," to the disgruntled ex-employee who targets her former boss, co-workers or the entire company.

The vengeful stalker sees himself as the victim and that their stalking is just "getting even" for past injustices.

The vengeful stalker can be more malicious and dangerous than the other two types of stalkers, since the others still mean to establish or re-establish a relationship, while the vengeful stalker is not interested in a relationship, he wants to punish the victim.

Intimate Partner Stalker: Well over half of all stalkers fall into this *"former intimate partner"* category.

These are typically men whose partners have ended the relationship and they refuse to let go. They may play the innocent, lovelorn victim to garner the sympathy and support from friends and family, but in reality, they are most likely psychopaths that were abusive and manipulative during the relationship. Their refusal to let go is not out of any sense of love because they are not *capable* of love. They refuse to let go because they believe the victim is their private property, subject to only their whims.

Defense Against Stalkers

If you become a victim of a stalker, your first line of defense is to build a support system for yourself. Also, go to a lawyer, as well as family, friends, co-workers, your boss and neighbors and let them know what is going on. Bear in mind that often, none of these avenues will be of any assistance, but you need to try because chances are you will not be able to handle the situation alone. By building a support system, you can bring other tools to bear on the situation, such as tactics and training, and security measures.

Tactics and Training*:* Your primary tactic in dealing with most psychopaths is to escape and cut the offender out of your life; period.

Remember, there is no reasoning, negotiating, or appealing to the sympathy of psychopaths or delusional individuals. You must say "No" once and then never speak to the stalker again. For stalkers, like obscene phone callers, even negative attention is STILL attention.

For the Vengeful Stalker, the same rule applies. When you encounter someone whose reaction to you is way out of proportion, simply back away.

Having no reaction at all is the best way to prevent adding any more fuel to the fire.

Remember, you are dealing with a lunatic; you gain nothing by counter-attacking at this point.

Take a self-defense course. This is different from martial arts training, which may or may not be geared to personal self-defense. A good self-defense course – such as the quarterly self-defense courses at the *Afrikan Martial Arts Institute* – can train you to be more aware and strategic in your thinking, which can aid you in dealing with a stalker.

Traditional, practical martial arts training, after taking a good self-defense course, will also benefit you. Of course, I recommend that you train at one of the branches of the Afrikan Martial Arts Institute. If you do not live near one of *our* branch schools, I recommend you find a reputable Filipino Kali/Arnis/Escrima school, or Indonesian Pecak Silat school – martial arts that continue their blade culture will help develop the strategic mindset you need and the calmness under pressure.

Also, carry a weapon, whenever you can as an equalizer. If you are concerned about the laws in this lawless society, carry pepper spray; it has varying degrees of effectiveness but is at least legally neutral in most places. However, depending on both the legalities and personal attitudes, more lethal weapons such as knives and firearms may be considered as well.

Personally, I recommend every adult carry two knives – one clipped inside the lower pocket and one clipped inside the boot, or strapped to the outer ankle area. If you are taken to the ground, getting to either knife will be simple enough. If you carry a knife or two, work on deploying the knife from wherever you carry it. To "deploy" means to draw the knife and have it ready for combat. You should be able to deploy any weapon in under a second. This takes constant practice.

Security Measures: Upgrade your home security by installing an alarm system, surveillance cameras, entry prevention devices and building a safe room. You might also want to get a dog. A dog is one of the least expensive, but most effective, alarm systems.

Block your address at DMV and Voter Registration. NEVER give out your home address or telephone number to strangers – businesses are strangers, too, by the way.

Get a post office box and use it on all correspondence. For those places that will not accept a post office box, simply change "PO Box" to "Apt." Put this address on your checks.

If you have a stalker, have co-workers screen all calls and visitors at your place of employment. Do not accept packages unless they were personally ordered. Remove any name or identification from reserved parking at work and destroy discarded mail.

Equip your gas tank with a locking gas cap that can be unlocked only from inside the car. Acquaint yourself with all-night stores and other public, highly populated places in your area. Keep a cell phone with you at all times, even inside your home, in case the stalker cuts your phone lines.

If you think you are being followed while in your car, make four left – or right – turns in succession. If the car continues to follow you, drive to the nearest gas station and phone comrades to meet you; do NOT go home or to a friend's house.

Consider moving if your case warrants it. No, it's not fair, but nothing is fair about stalking. If you stay and fight through the legal system, you *might* get some justice, but you almost certainly will not get safety.

Restraining Orders*:* Many people believe that if they are being stalked the first thing they should do is get a restraining order, better known as a TRO – temporary restraining order. People often assume that by doing so, the stalking will finally end, either because the stalker will stop on his or her own, or because the police will stop him or her. Neither of these outcomes are likely.

Only about half of all stalking cases are reported to the police and of these, only 25% result in an arrest. About a quarter of stalking victims obtain restraining orders; nearly 70% of those restraining order are violated.

A restraining order does not provide police protection – and rarely police action – when it is violated. Furthermore, the likelihood of police preventing a stalker from attacking you is close to zero.

While a restraining order does little to stop the stalker, and *nothing* to prevent an attack, it *can* have a NEGATIVE effect:

Because of a psychopath's grandiose ego, *a restraining order is often seen as an open rejection and declaration of war.* The restraining order is a direct attack, and the psychopath is again the victim, for which he quickly becomes the vengeful type stalker, bent on punishing the wrong doer.

Restraining orders are most likely to be violated by the delusional and intimate partner-type of stalkers. Delusional stalkers, by definition, cannot be reasoned with. They just do not get it and never will. A court order is just a piece of paper to them.

Former intimate partner stalkers are less likely to adhere to a restraining order the more they have invested in the victim. They feel that nothing should interfere with them retrieving the debt they think their victim owes them.

Children's Safety & Self Defense

Self-defense for children is the responsibility of every parent. It is so simple to teach children a few lifesaving crime prevention and survival skills that there is no excuse not to do so. Parents should begin to teach basic survival knowledge as soon as the child is old enough to understand and respond to instruction.

In the beginning, teach simple skills such as having your child(ren) memorize their home address and telephone number. As they mature, teach them what to do if they become lost, or have to stay alone in the home. This should be a continuous and on-going educational program.

What to Teach Children

- Their home address and telephone number (including area code) as soon as it is possible for them to learn

- Phone numbers where parents can be reached when they are not at home, or a trusted neighbor or relative that they can call for help

- How to reach you in an emergency

- Make sure that your child understands that adults do not keep secrets with children

- That it is all right to say "no" to an adult if the adult wants them to do something you have taught them is wrong

- That no one has the right to touch any part of his or her body

- To tell you if someone has asked them to keep a secret from you

- To report anyone who exposes their private parts to you. Tell school authorities, and/or trusted family.

House Rules

Establish and explain to your children a set of house safety rules. These should include:

- If someone knocks on the door, do not open it. Only let those people in that parents have approved. If anyone else tries to come in, call trusted comrades from a list that you provide

- In the event of a fire, or if the smoke detector goes off, leave the house immediately. Go to a trusted neighbor's house, and call 911 for the Fire Department

- In the event of an emergency, call you at work, or call a trusted neighbor, or comrade

- Never say they are alone if they answer the phone

- Have your child call when they get home so you will not worry

- Make sure your children can reach the phone. Put a list of your work, trusted neighbors, and emergency numbers near the phone.

Rules for Going Out

In addition to safety rules for the home, also institute the following safety rules for children when they go out.

- Tell you where they will be at all times

- Do not enter anyone's home, or isolated areas, without your permission

- Do not accept gifts or treats from strangers

- Never approach or enter a stranger's car; move away from a car that pulls up beside them if they do not know the driver

- Never take shortcuts through empty parks, fields, or isolated areas

- If they are being followed, they should run home or go to the nearest public place and yell for help

- Always travel in pairs, or in groups with more mature children

- If they become separated from you at a grocery store or shopping mall, go directly to a cashier

What Parents Should Know

- Develop a password with your children; tell them if anyone ever claims they were sent by you to pick them up, that person must give them the password

- Know where your children are, whom they are with, and when you expect them home.

- Make a point of knowing who their friends are, where their friends live, and write down their friends' telephone numbers

- Do not allow your children to wear their names on T-shirts, lunch boxes, jackets or jewelry in public. A child is likely to trust someone who addresses him or her by name

- Do not provide personal information about your children on surveys and questionnaires unless a very good reason is given.

- Make sure you are familiar with all baby-sitters. Check their references

- Always accompany children to the bathroom in a public place, and advise them never to loiter in or around the area.

- Create and keep a child identity kit

Child Identity Kit

A child identity kit contains important information on each of your children that can be vital to search efforts in the event your child goes missing.

The kit should contain:

- An up-to-date color photograph of each child. Update the photo at least once a year

- Vital stats, such as name, age, birth date, hair color, eye color, height and weight

- Any medical conditions, such as asthma or allergies

All of this information should be placed on a single sheet of paper or card so that it can be easily photocopied or scanned and sent out to searchers should your child go missing.

What To Do If A Child Is Missing

If your child goes missing:

- Make a careful search of your home and surrounding property

- Check with playmates

- Check favorite play areas

- Call all friends, neighbors, and relatives

Defense Against Child Abduction

All predators, both in the wild and in society, will only pursue prey as long as the caloric gains exceed the caloric expenditures.

Criminals will engage in criminal activity only for as long as the perceived benefits outweigh the perceived risks. Time is the enemy of criminals since the longer it takes to commit a crime, the greater the risk of capture.

The *Afrikan Martial Arts Institute* teaches children to become extremely difficult to handle so that a predator would need to expend extra time and energy during the attack stage. Although there is nothing a child could do to prevent a determined adult from carrying them away, the longer a child can delay the predator, and the greater commotion that child can cause, the riskier it becomes and thus more likely for the predator to break off the attack.

The *Afrikan Martial Arts Institute* teaches children that if anyone grabs a hold of them and tries to take them away, they should do the following:

- First, they should drop to the ground, this is to make them a dead weight and more difficult to drag or carry away.

- Next, they should position their body so that their feet are towards the attacker and kick out at the shins of the attacker.

- Then, make as much noise as possible while yelling "No! Leave me alone! You're not my mommy; you're not my daddy. Somebody, HELP!"

Finally, if the attacker is still holding on, they should bite the hand holding them, or execute an escape technique from the wrist or collar grab.

CHAPTER EIGHT
POLICE & LAW ENFORCEMENT

Dangers of Dealing With The Police

In an ideal society, the police are public servants that prevent crime or capture and punish the criminal after the act. However, America is NOT an ideal society. It never has been. Even the most effective police forces throughout the world seldom *prevent* crime.

Capturing the criminal afterwards is a distant concern for the victims of rape, assault and other violent crime. This is why it is essential for everyone to learn crime prevention strategies, since relying on the police for protection is a statistically foolish gamble.

Like any other gang or hunting party, police forces are a mob of armed men and women. The police – be they city, county, state, or federal employees – are ALWAYS dangerous, for a number of reasons:

First, armed mobs are more likely to resort to force and violence. Weapons can instantly escalate misunderstandings and miscommunication to lethal levels.

Second, the gang mentality of a police force tends to create a strong "Us-and-Them" culture, in which anyone not a member of the authoritarian hierarchy is automatically a criminal. When this mindset predominates, innocent people are arrested, imprisoned, abused and often murdered.

Finally, the power, authority, protection, and special privileges afforded by membership in a police force attract psychopaths. Throughout history and in many different cultures, police forces are as corrupt and dangerous as the most notorious organized crime families. In addition, when a nation's government becomes dominated by psychopathic personalities they always seek to transform local police forces into what amounts to an occupation army to be used against civilians.

To complicate matters even more, many psychopaths have impersonated police officers in order to get their victim's compliance and lure them into a trap. For the above reasons, you should always approach and deal with the police with caution, if you must deal with them at all.

Dealing With The Police

There are three basic types of encounters with the police: *Conversation, Detention,* and *Arrest.* All are dangerous and can lead to your incarceration, incapacitation, or death:

Conversation: If the police are trying to get information, but do not have enough evidence to detain or arrest you, they may try to obtain information by starting a "friendly conversation." If you talk to them, you may give them the information they need to arrest you or your friends and comrades. Whenever a law official asks you *anything*, it is legally safest not to answer any questions. Ask if you are being detained. If not, you can *legally* leave and say nothing else to them.

Note, I put an emphasis on legally. Of course, when dealing with the lawless – they are NOT the "law," in my opinion – they don't care about legalities. Caucasians can pull this off. Most times, YOU, my dear Afrikan and Indigenous brothers and sisters, cannot. To them, YOU not answering their questions is the slave not answering the slavemaster and those psychopaths will seek to punish you for your "insolence."

If you opt to leave, be prepared to fight for your life; or, at best, run, like Usain Bolt after a White woman.

Never agree to go to the police station for questioning. Simply say, "I don't know anything."

No matter how you may feel about being stopped or inconvenienced, never bad-mouth a police officer. Stay calm and in control of your words, body langauge and your emotions.

Detention: Police are *supposed* to detain you only if they have reasonable suspicion that you are involved in a crime. Detention means that, though you are not arrested, you cannot leave. Detention is *supposed* to last a short time and they are not *supposed* to move you. During detention, the police will pat you down and search your belongings. They are not *supposed* to go into your pockets unless they feel a weapon. Note my emphasis again – the lawless do NOT care about the law...except how that law serves and protects THEM.

Police have two reasons to detain you:

1. They are writing you a citation, such as a traffic ticket

2. They want to arrest you, but they do not have enough information yet to do so.

A detention can easily lead to arrest. If the police are detaining you and they get information that you are involved in a crime, they will arrest you, even if it has nothing to do with your detention. For example, if you are pulled over for speeding – i.e., detained – and the officer sees a joint in the car, he or she can arrest you for possession of drugs even though that is not the reason you were pulled over in the first place.

If you are detained, the police are allowed, by law, to pat down or frisk your outer clothing to see if you have any weapons. If the police officer feels something that could be a weapon, then he can go into your pockets and pull out the suspicious item. Otherwise, a police officer is not *supposed* to go through your pockets or tell you to empty your pockets. By law, the only time a police officer can go through your pockets is if you are under arrest.

Never consent to a search. If the police try to search your house, car, backpack, pockets, etc. say, "I do not consent to this search." This may not stop them from forcing their way in and searching anyway, but if they search you illegally, they may not be able to use the evidence against you in court. To protect yourself make it clear that you do not consent to a search and ask the police officer why he is searching you.

Arrest

Police can arrest you only if they have probable cause that you are involved in a crime. This means the police must be able to describe criminal related behavior based on what can be observed. They are not *supposed* to just stop someone because they do not like the way the person looks, they are *supposed* to be more specific. For example, if there was a robbery at a nearby store and you are seen walking away from the scene, this is not *supposed* to be enough to arrest you.

In theory, probable cause is the criteria under which the police can arrest someone; in reality, the police arrest anyone, anywhere, for any reason they like.

Remember: the police *do not* decide your charges. They can only make recommendations. The *prosecutor* is the only person who can actually charge you. Remember this if you are ever threatened by police rattling off all the charges they are supposedly "going to give you."

If the police knock and ask to enter your home, you do not have to open the door unless they have a warrant signed by a judge. Letting police into your home voluntarily means that your encounter with them will likely last longer, and they can also look for, and plant, evidence of criminal activity. The judicial codes of most countries are so bloated that practically everyone is guilty of some criminal offense at any time.

If the police come to your door with an arrest warrant, go outside and lock the door behind you. If you go back into the house for any reason they can follow you in and search any room you go into.

If they have an arrest warrant, they are allowed to force their way in if they know you are in there.

In some emergencies such as when a person is screaming for help inside a home, or if someone has called 911 from that address, officers are allowed to enter and search the home without a warrant. Note: if YOU call the police on someone at your address, you have also given the police permission to search your home. If they find something they can pin on you as evidence of a crime, YOU will probably go to jail right along with the person you called the police on.

When you are arrested, the police can search you to the skin and go through your car and any belongings. By law, an officer who strip-searches you must be the same gender as you.

Miranda Rights

A Miranda warning is a warning given by police in the United States to criminal suspects in police custody, or in a custodial situation, before they are interrogated. There are variations of what is exactly spoken but generally the warning is as follows:

"You have the right to remain silent. Anything you say or do can and will be used against you in a court of law. You have the right to an attorney. If you cannot afford an attorney, one will be appointed to you. Do you understand these rights as they have been read to you?"

In Canada, equivalent rights exist under the *Charter of Rights and Freedoms*. The Canadian Charter warning reads as follows:

"You are under arrest for _____ (charge), do you understand? You have the right to retain and instruct counsel without delay. We will provide you with a toll-free telephone lawyer referral service, if you do not have your own lawyer. Anything you say can be used in court as evidence. Do you understand? Would you like to speak to a lawyer?"

England, Australia, New Zealand, Europe and most other so-called "developed" countries have similar rights.

Interrogation

The police are *supposed* to read you your Miranda rights (also known as the Miranda warnings) whenever there is an interrogation by a police officer or other agent of law enforcement while you are in custody. An officer may handcuff you or put you in the back of a police cruiser placing you "in custody" before you are formally arrested. Even if you have not been read your rights, what you say can - and WILL – be used against you.

Knowing your rights and demanding them won't help you much against the lawless, though and can even endanger you. Many police officers become aggressive and hostile if they think you "know your rights." Police often use intimidation to make suspects nervous and more cooperative.

Standing up for your rights might get you beaten up or killed. Your rights are not something you can realistically depend on when locked in a windowless room with no witnesses. Police are armed psychopaths with virtual impunity to use those weapons. They are the most dangerous members of our society. Always be cautious when you talk to them and do your best to avoid EVER being taken into custody.

Common ploys to make you talk:

- "You will have to stay here and answer my questions" or "You're not leaving until I find out what I want."

- "I have evidence on you. Tell me what I want to know or else." (They can present fake evidence to convince you to tell them what they want to know).

- "You are not a suspect; we're simply investigating, so just help us understand what happened and then you can go."

- "If you don't answer my questions, I won't have any choice but to take you to jail."

- "If you don't answer these questions, you'll be charged with resisting arrest."

- "All of your friends have cooperated and we let them go home; you are the only one left."

- "All of your friends have cooperated with us for lighter sentences and you will take the full brunt of the charges, unless you cooperate as well."

- "We already know what you did, so confess or face worse consequences."

No knock Warrant

In the U.S., a no knock warrant is a warrant issued by a judge that allows law enforcement officers to enter a property without knocking and without identifying themselves as police. It is issued under the belief that any evidence they hope to find can be destroyed during the time that police identify themselves and the time they secure the area.

Having armed men wearing black masks that do not identify themselves as police and who break down your door is a terrifying experience. Many innocent people have been murdered by the police when they thought criminals were invading their homes and they sought to defend themselves.

Undercover And Secret Police

When psychopaths dominate the government of a country, they inevitably use the police as the enforcement arm of the political machine. Anyone that disagrees or disapproves of a government's criminal activities automatically becomes a criminal, subversive, or "terrorist."

The enforcement of political compliance is usually carried out by "special" law enforcement agencies that work under varying degrees of secrecy, hence the "secret police." In the U.S., these would be the FBI, INS, NSA, CIA, Homeland Security and a host of other clandestine forces. In the U.K., this would include MI5, MI6, and Scotland Yard. Each country has its own version of the secret police, each with varying degrees of secrecy.

Ostensibly, these law enforcement agencies are chartered to prevent international criminals from operating within the country and/or counter espionage and counter-terrorism functions. In reality, each secret police force found in every country in the world has been used to investigate their own citizens' political and social activities, despite the fact that these activities are protected by the constitutions of their countries.

You may think that if you do not belong to some radical or subversive political group you do not have to worry about being arrested by the secret police, however, this is incorrect. Almost any group or organization can be deemed a threat by the authorities, politicized, and become targets of the secret police. These include unions, craft guilds, community service groups, charities, protest and environmental groups, gun and sports clubs, religious groups, advocacy organizations, and political parties – all such groups have been targeted at one time or another by their own governments' secret police.

Often, you may be completely unaware that your group or organization is under investigation until after you are arrested. It does not matter whether, in fact, your group is politically subversive or even politically aware for you to be targeted for reasons that may be incomprehensible. For example, a group of vegans, comprised of homemakers and public school teachers that are working to build a garden and raise chickens in a vacant lot in the Bankhead area of Atlanta may seem the most innocent of organizations. However, if a corrupt government official has already signed a deal with a corrupt corporation to exploit the vacant lot in question, then these homemakers and teachers automatically become "subversives." Undercover police will be sent in to investigate and then sabotage the group using the typical tools of intimidation, extortion, and subversion.

Undercover/secret police can lie about anything they please including about being police, even if asked directly. Undercover police can even break the law and encourage others to do so as well. For example, undercover narcotics officers get hazard pay for doing drugs as part of their cover. If an undercover agent manages to convince some or all members of your group to commit increasingly criminal activities then the group is soon to be arrested. In a worst-case scenario, the undercover officers may plant evidence and provide false testimony.

Defense Against The Secret Police

Beware of new members that join your organization, especially if they seem to have unusual resources and are advocating a more radical or violent approach. For example, undercover police have been used to mingle among peaceful protesters to throw rocks and commit violence and vandalism in order to discredit and criminalize the peaceful protestors.

An undercover officer may introduce drugs or weapons into your organization and should any of your members avail themselves of these items they endanger the entire organization. Isolate, expel, or disassociate any new members immediately upon the first instance of criminal activity.

If you suspect you or your organization may become a target of political intrigue and persecution, pool the groups' resources and retain a law firm that specializes in defending against civil rights violations. Make sure all members have and carry the firm's contact information with them.

If any member of your group is approached or arrested by the police, he or she should, as soon as possible, notify all other members. Make sure everyone understands his or her civil rights and how to safely deal with police contact.

Whenever you interact with or observe the police, keep a record. Write down what is said and who said it. Write down the officers' names, badge numbers, and the names and contact information of any witnesses. Record everything that happens.

If you or your organization is being subjected to a harassment campaign by police, then carry a small tape recorder or video camera with you and record your encounters with them. Be discreet. Most police do not like being recorded or filmed, especially if they are planning to violate your civil rights. Recording police actions may cause them to respond aggressively and seize or destroy your recording equipment. However, if there are more witnesses around, someone can record the police's brutal actions. It is important to know your legal rights, but it is also important for you to decide when and how to use them to protect yourself.

Make sure that when you are arrested with other people, the rest of the group knows their right to remain silent. If anyone breaks and talks, you all go down.

Incarceration

Remember that if you are arrested and cannot afford an attorney, you have the right to a public defender. Just know that the public defender works for the same White Supremacist System that arrested you in the first place.

Within a reasonable time after your arrest, or booking, you have the right to make a local phone call: to a lawyer, bail bondsman, a relative or any other person. The police are not *supposed* to listen to the call to the lawyer. If you are on probation or parole, tell your parole office you have been arrested, but nothing else.

Do not talk to the inmates in jail about your case. They could be informants or undercover officers and your jailhouse talk could be used against you in a court of law.

You may be released, with or without bail, following the booking. If not, you have the right to go into court and see a judge the next court day after your arrest. Demand this right! When you appear before the judge, ask for an attorney. An attorney has a better chance at convincing a judge to let you out on a lower bail than you could.

If A Friend Or Family Member Has Been Arrested

If you get a call from a police officer or a friend or family member saying that he or she has been arrested and incarcerated the first things you need to know are; where they are being held, by what police agency, and what the actual charge is.

If you are speaking with your friend, tell him or her that you are finding a lawyer and then warn them not to answer any questions or make any statements until that lawyer arrives. Do not discuss any details of the alleged crime over the phone since anything they say, even to you over the phone, can be used against them in court. If the arrested is an adult, the police are not required to tell a friend or family member anything.

Find a criminal defense attorney. If you have a family or business attorney you already use then get him or her to recommend a good defense attorney for you. Having another lawyer refer you helps your credibility and the defense attorney may not require as much money up-front than if you just cold called them. If not, then search the internet and/or yellow pages for one nearest you or the place your friend is being incarcerated. Brief the lawyer on the situation, including the address of the police station.

Gather as much money as you can to pay the lawyer and to post bail. It is important to get a good lawyer on the case early. Once a lawyer has been retained, follow his or her directions, but do not relinquish critical thinking and common sense. If you feel there is something wrong about the defense proceedings, get another opinion. If need be, fire the attorney and hire another.

CHAPTER NINE
WEAPONS

No study of survival, preparedness and self-defense is complete without a rudimentary knowledge of weaponry, since it is often a weapon that determines combat and survival strategy and tactics.

As a rule, a weapon is preferable to your empty hands in a struggle for survival. However, carrying a weapon for self-defense has several drawbacks. The first is accessibility. Unless the weapon is carried in the hand, you may not be able to retrieve it from a purse, pocket, boot, or waistband in time to use it. Criminals use the element of surprise, which means there may be no time to go for your weapon.

Another drawback is the skill required to use a weapon effectively. While traditional Asian martial arts weapons such as nunchakus, kobutans, sais and samurai swords appear lethal in the Dojo and in movies, under the stress of a street fight, they can be awkward and difficult to handle.

A weapon is a tool used to accomplish an objective. The most important tools at your disposal are your mind, and your senses. However, you may also need to resort to the use of weaponry. Below are different types of weapons according to their classification as *Commercial Weapons*, *Improvised Weapons* and *Anatomical Weapons*.

Commercial Weapons

Self-Defense Sprays: There are several types of chemical spray dispensers that employ a variety of chemicals. Commonly labeled *pepper spray*, they are marketed as self-defense against dogs, bears, and humans.

The advantage to carrying a pepper spray device is that it is inexpensive, requires no training, and is legal in most areas – however, they are not allowed on airplanes. They can be effective at keeping an attacker at a safe distance.

The drawbacks are they may not work on someone that is on drugs, in a psychotic rage, has a high tolerance to pain, or who regularly eats high amounts of very hot pepper – like I do.

When choosing a spray unit, there are three important factors to consider:

One consideration is the type of medium – liquid, or foam. I recommend foam, as foam is less likely to be dispersed by the wind, or worse, blown back into your face, which sometimes happens with the liquid. The foam is effective at a distance of 4 to 6 feet.

Another consideration is the spray pattern with the liquid medium. There are two types – one shoots a stream, and the other shoots a cone of mist.

With the stream dispensers, you get greater distance – 15 to 20 feet – and they are more effective under windy conditions, but you need to be more precise in aiming.

The mist spray has a shorter range – 4 to 6 feet – and is easily blown away by the wind, but is easier to aim.

The final factor is the trigger mechanism and/or size of the unit. Choose a model that you can easily fit in a pocket or handbag and that when you grab it, you can tell instantly which direction the nozzle is pointing without having to look at it.

Like any weapon, pepper spray – also known as oleo capsicum – is only effective if you can employ it successfully. If you are traveling through a high-risk area such as an empty parking garage, or poorly lit street at night, then carry the spray in your hand and keep your hand hidden in a pocket. Also, keep it handy when you are driving.

Spray into the eyes of an attacker and while he or she is adjusting to the pain and watery eyes, use that opportunity to run to safety, or to deliver an incapacitating strike.

Stun Guns and Tasers: Stun guns are handheld electronic devices that work by sending an electrical charge through an attacker that temporarily disrupts his nervous system. They typically have two or four electrodes that must make physical contact with the attacker in order to work.

The advantage to using a stun gun is that they require no training to use and can incapacitate an attacker under ideal conditions.

The drawbacks are they are illegal in most areas, and like pepper spray, may not work all the time. Since you are required to make contact with your attacker to employ it, there is a greater risk involved in their use.

Tasers are stun guns that also shoot out two small darts attacked to wires to a distance of about fifteen to twenty feet. These darts penetrate the attacker and then deliver the shock from a safe distance.

Disadvantages of the Taser are they are expensive, illegal, and they are a one shot weapon. If you miss or there are multiple attackers, then they work like any other stun gun with the same drawbacks.

Impact Weapons: There are several types of commercially made impact weapons such as police batons, extendable steel batons, and heavy-duty flashlights.

The advantage is their low cost, easy availability and effectiveness in causing serious structural damage to an attacker. Swinging a club is an almost instinctive skill so most will be able to wield a baton effectively.

The disadvantage is that you need to be close to the attacker. If you plan to use an impact weapon for self-defense, at a minimum, you should take a workshop in their use.

Edged Weapons: Knives are inexpensive, easily available, easily concealed and, in most instances, legal to carry.

Knives require less strength to use than impact weapons and even a small person can inflict incapacitating wounds with one. A knife is also a useful tool in a disaster/survival situation.

The drawback, again, is the fact that you have to close with an attacker to employ a blade. To be truly effective, some training is a must, and knowledge of anatomy helps, too. In the hands of a trained person, a knife is the most dangerous weapon you will encounter in most settings.

Since, in many areas carrying a knife with a blade of five inches or longer is illegal, the best bet for a knife to carry on your person in an urban setting is a locking, folding knife with a blade between two to four inches in length. Purchase one with a thumbscrew that allows you to open the blade with one hand and a locking mechanism – a vital safety feature that prevents the knife from folding back onto your fingers during a struggle.

Personally, I prefer carrying fixed blade knives for faster deployment, but a *good* fixed blade knife is much more expensive than a *great* folding knife.

Firearms: Firearms are the best self-defense weapon *in terms of intimidation and stopping an attacker from a distance.*

In many cases, simply presenting the firearm will prevent an attack.

As with all weapons, there are disadvantages. Firearms are heavily regulated everywhere in the world, and illegal in most places. Extreme care must be taken when using a firearm, since even slight miscalculations can maim or kill an innocent person. In addition, they are lethal weapons, in that you cannot just use pain or discomfort to stop someone, you must be prepared to kill the attacker and deal with the legal and emotional consequences afterwards.

If you are able to acquire a firearm, then you also need to be properly trained on how to use it in a defensive scenario and then maintain proficiency through regular practice.

- *Handguns:* Handguns are small, easy to conceal and carry, and ideally suited for close quarters combat. However, handguns require the most practice of any firearm to use effectively and safely. There are a wide range of handguns; choosing one that is right for you requires time and effort to learn what the options are and what will be the best handgun for you.

- *Shotguns:* If you live in an urban area where owning a handgun is illegal, your next option is usually a long arm, such as a rifle or shotgun. Shotguns are available in many jurisdictions where every other firearm is illegal. The advantages a shotgun has over other firearms are its stopping power and versatility. Shotguns have the most stopping power against man-sized targets than any other firearm at effective range. Also the wide variety of shell loads allow the shotgun to be used in many application from bird and game hunting to sports like trap and skeet shooting.

  Shotguns are typically effective up to 50 yards, which is adequate in an urban home self-defense scenario. The drawbacks to the shotgun include its limited range and accuracy compared to rifles. They also have a strong recoil that intimidates many novice shooters.

- *Rifles:* Rifles are much easier to shoot than any other firearm. They are easier to aim, lighter, and have less recoil than a shotgun. The drawback in a self-defense scenario is the penetrating power of rifle rounds, which can easily penetrate walls and doors and travel up to a mile, possibly injuring innocent people. They are usually longer than a shotgun and thus even more unwieldy in a cramped urban self-defense scenario.

Finally, shotguns and rifles are strictly home defense weapons; you cannot go to the mall with a sniper rifle slung over your shoulder.

Improvised Weapons

In a life or death battle, a weapon, *any* weapon, will help to improve your odds of survival. If you are unable to acquire a commercial weapon, or the one you have is unavailable to you at the moment, then your best option is to improvise one.

The following briefly describe ways of improvising and using an assortment of everyday items as weapons.

Penetrating Weapons

These weapons cause injury by piercing the skin and/or body cavities. Classical examples include stabbing weapons such as swords, spears, and daggers.

- *Pen, Kobutan, Small Stick:* Held tightly in the fist, any solid tubular object can deliver serious destructive energy with no injury to the hand. A four to six inch piece of doweling, pipe, tubing, or such everyday objects as pens, markers, or lighters can be used. Use such improvised weapons the same way you would use an ice-pick, stabbing to the temples, the soft areas of the face, the neck and the groin.

- *Umbrella, Walking Stick:* Instinct says to use these as bludgeoning weapons, but these are more lethal when used in a two handed thrusting motion. The narrow metal tip found on most umbrellas can penetrate clothing, skin, and muscles like a sword. Targets include the solar plexus, temples, and throat. Use the center section of the umbrella or cane – the portion between your hands when you hold it with both of them – to block incoming attacks and to thrust, horizontally, against the throat.

Cutting Weapons

A sharp edge is used to inflict damage by slicing sinew and blood vessels, which may stop an attacker due to loss of blood, intimidation at the sight of blood, or impairment of physical functions by cutting major blood vessels and tendons. Traditional cutting weapons include the knife, sword, axe, and halberd. Most kitchen knives are just as lethal as fighting knives and are more readily available.

- *Keys:* Held in the fist with the pointed ends of the keys protruding between the fingers, they can be used to scratch and cut. Directed towards the face, the wounds themselves would not be serious enough to stop an attacker, but the blood from facial wounds can blind and distract the attacker.

- *Broken Glass:* Using a broken bottle top as a cutting weapon is a cliché, but beware – bottles are more difficult to break than you think. Make sure you hit it against a hard surface to break it. This weapon is only useful for intimidation purposes since its slippery grip, irregular shape, and fragility, makes it an unreliable weapon. A bottle makes a better projectile or club.

Bludgeoning Weapons

These weapons rely on their mass to generate force and inflict damage. Classical bludgeons include man's first improvised weapon – the club and its more evolved descendants, the mace and war hammer.

Bludgeoning weapons are difficult to block against since their strategy is to smash through a person's defense. Bludgeoning weapons require little skill to use effectively and are therefore more suitable for those with little training.

- *Baseball Bat, Tire Iron, Metal Pipes:* One or more of these can usually be found around the house. The basic method is to simply grasp the weapon in both hands and swing against an attacker without any specific target. The baseball bat is one of the best weapons for home self-defense, especially for women since it is light enough to swing easily but solid enough to injure a larger attacker. Keep one under the bed and another beside the front door.

- *Stick, Cane, Broom Handle:* Best used either in a thrusting manner, like a spear, or laterally, holding both ends to "clothesline" an attacker's throat.

  Another method is to hold the stick in one hand and whirl the stick in a circular 'figure-eight' pattern to intimidate attackers. However, a stick, in the hands of an untrained person, is usually too light to have real stopping power. The average person can easily take a hit from a stick without suffering debilitating pain or injury. Extensive training in stick fighting greatly increases a stick's effectiveness as a weapon.

- *Rolled Magazine:* Tightly roll a magazine into a tube and grasp it firmly in your fist with the bottom of the tube protruding about an inch from the bottom of the fist. The tightly compressed paper around the butt end is solid enough to deliver a heavy blow. This improvised weapon is most effective when you use the butt end in a hammering action aimed at the bridge of the nose, temple, back of the neck or collarbone. The forward end can be thrust at the eyes, throat, or groin, or in a striking action, like swatting a fly, to the nose and ears.

- *Bottles and Bar Stools:* When you are in a restaurant or a bar, these are readily available weapons. A bottle makes an effective club and a chair or stool is effective and against multiple attackers. Don't swing a chair or stool over your head, since this would leave you wide open to a tackle; use them to thrust, like a lion tamer, to keep your attackers at bay as you carefully back-out of the situation.

Flexible Weapons

Flexible weapons deliver destructive force through speed that can crush or cut. Classical flexible weapons include flails, whips, and weighted chains. The biggest advantage to flexible weapons is that they are difficult to block since their flexibility allows the weapon to whip around a block to strike from the side and even from behind. There are several ways to improvise flails and whips.

- *Belt and Buckle, Dog Leash, Key Chain:* With a belt, wrap the end around the fist once to make a tight grip and use the weight of the buckle as a flail. With a piece of rope, tie a couple of knots at one end to act as a weight. With chains, such as a dog leash or a key ring and chain combination, again, wrap one end around the fist and use the heaviest end to swing at assailants. The basic method of using flexible weapons is to use swinging strikes. Another tactic is to swing the weapon in a whirling figure-eight pattern in front of your body to drive back or discourage an attacker.

- *Sock, Pantyhose, Stocking, Wool Ski Hat, Pillowcase:* Any of these can be stuffed with something solid such as; loose change, a can of soda, or a handful of stones. Hold it tightly by the open end and swing it around as a flail. With lighter material, such as socks and pantyhose first tie a knot at the toe-end before adding the weight, this provides a little more strength so that the weight does not rip through the fabric on the first strike.

- *Purse, Briefcase, Gym Bag, Backpack:* These make somewhat larger and slower flails but their extra weight compensates for the lack of speed. Grasp by the handles and swing in an arching motion against the attacker's head. For a heavier impact, carry a hardcover book in your purse or school bag, or a pair of shoes in your gym bag. These also make fairly good shields against impact and edged weapons, especially with a hardcover book inside it.

Throwing Weapons

Among the Yoruba of West Afrika, Sango, the hero and Orisa (Force of Nature) of Thunder, is called Jakuta – the Stone Thrower – because one of his favored weapons are smooth, heavy stones that he throws at his enemies. This tells us that among the Yoruba, stone throwing is an honored skill.

As primitive as this may seem, the stone-throwers, at close range, were accurate and effective in stopping even armor-clad infantry and cavalry.

Though less lethal than arrows, stone throwers compensate for this with a rate of fire three to four times that of archers. Against larger or multiple attackers this ancient tactic can be surprisingly effective; simply pick up as many objects as you can and throw them at your attacker.

Common objects that make handy projectiles include rocks, dirt, sand, bottles, ashtrays, salt-and-pepper shakers, soda cans, furniture, and shoes.

Chemical Weapons

Most chemical weapons irritate the eyes and the mucus membrane tissues in the nose, mouth, throat, and lungs.

Chemicals are administered through either a spray or a powder that is aimed at the face. Commercial self-defense chemicals include pepper spray and mace. However, when these are unavailable, some items found around the house can be used as chemical weapons:

- ***Irritant Powders:*** Common irritant powders include salt, pepper, chili powder, drain cleaners, and sand.

These can be secretly carried in the hand or a pocket and thrown, at close-range, into the face to temporarily blind an attacker.

- **Spray Paint:** A can of oil-based spray paint will irritate the eyes and throat as well as mark and identify the attacker.

  A florescent color is best, since it will attract unwanted attention to the attacker. Once marked, it is hoped that an attacker will be more concerned about scrubbing off the telltale paint than continuing the attack.

Fire Weapons

Fire is one of man's oldest weapons and there are numerous variations in its use. The most common tactic is the use of fire as a distraction in order to escape. Set fire to something of value to your opponent and he will break off his attack to rescue the items from destruction. A fire is something that cannot be ignored. Below are a few fire weapons:

- **Gasoline and Match:** Throw a glass of highly flammable liquid such as gasoline, paint thinner, or lighter fluid onto the attacker and then ignite a lighter or match; the attacker will be afraid to come any closer to you.

- **Aerosol Can Torch:** Many aerosol hair sprays, air fresheners, and the like contain flammable liquids. Holding a lit match or lighter two to three inches away from and below the nozzle as you spray it will ignite the liquid, creating a short-range flamethrower.

Use only short bursts, being careful to keep the flame away from the nozzle so that the heat will not melt the plastic tip.

- **Boiling Water:** Traditionally thrown over a parapet onto besiegers, it can also be used in home defense. If you are trapped in the bathroom, you can run the hot water until it is smoking hot and then fill a bowl or other container. Should the attacker succeed in breaking through the door, throw the water on him and take advantage of his shock and surprise to counter-attack and escape.

Anatomical Weapons

Compared to the teeth and claws of other predators, man's anatomical arsenal may seem inferior, however, our lack of weaponry is more than compensated for by the ingenious methods of turning almost every part of our anatomy into a weapon.

Martial arts teach that the body is itself a weapon. Science has shown that the hand of a martial arts expert can develop a peak velocity of 11 to 15 yards per second – even the average person can move their hand faster than a King Cobra can strike.

The *rupture modulus*, or breaking point, of human bone is more than forty times that of concrete and is thus capable of shattering wood and concrete. The following will examine some anatomical weapons, and give a brief description of their general application:

Head:

- Weighs approximately eight pounds and can deliver a devastating blow because of its size and mass.

- The best technique to use with the head is a head-butt: drop your chin to your chest and then use the side of the head, just above the level of the hairline, as a striking surface.

  Target the nose; a head-butt will break the delicate cartilage and cause extreme pain, bleeding, and watering of the eyes.

  A head-butt is often used as a type of "sucker punch," since the hands can be held relaxed at the sides to reduce suspicion. The head butt is also effective when grappling and both your, and your opponent's arms, are neutralized.

Shoulder:

- Can be used in a forward "tackle" technique, using the upper side as a striking surface to crack ribs and knock the wind out of an opponent.

- Can be used in a sideways motion, using the outside of the shoulder, to knock an opponent off his feet or crush him against a solid object.

- The drawbacks are its short range and limited application.

Elbows:

- Because of its solid boney structure, the elbow can deliver a powerful blow, easily capable of fracturing bones and rupturing internal organs.

- Used offensively, the elbow can be swung in an arching movement to strike forward or backward, as well as to the side.

- Used defensively, the elbows are held in close to the body to defend against attacks to the ribs and abdomen, or held close to the face to absorb attacks to the head and neck.

- Broken hands, feet, and shinbones are common injuries that occur when an opponent's attack lands against the hard bone of an elbow instead of the intended target.

Forearms:

- Can be used in both defensive and offensive roles.

- In defense, the forearms block or deflect incoming attacks.

- As an offensive weapon, the outside edge of the forearms, along the ulna bone, can be used in a chopping action against an opponent's arms when he attacks, or to strike at the ribs, throat and neck. Using the upper forearm (along the radius bone), the forearm can be used in a sweeping or "clothesline technique against the throat, or against the back or side of the neck.

Fist:

- A quick and effective weapon.

- Used against soft tissue targets, such as the nose, tip of the jaw, and solar plexus.

- Used as a setup for finishing techniques.

- There are two targets you should never punch: the head, and the mouth. The thickness and mass of the skull is sufficient to break the bones in the hand, while a punch to the mouth often results in the opponent's teeth severely cutting the hand; the human saliva in the resultant wounds are more likely to cause a serious infection.

  This happened to a close comrade and friend of mine when he punched a guy, known to eat mushrooms off the walls of abandoned buildings, in the mouth. The resultant infection landed him in the hospital.

Knee:

- The heavy bone structure of the knee makes it a powerful weapon. Even children can inflict severe pain and injury against a much larger attacker using the knee as a weapon.

- Traditional targets are the groin, the inside or outside of the thigh, and the face as a defense against a double-leg or single-leg takedown.

Feet:

- Several parts of the foot can be used as a striking surface – the ball, ridge, heel, and instep, all heavily boned surfaces that can deliver crushing strikes.

- Able to generate more power, and have a longer range than the feet.

- Have one major disadvantage: you sacrifice stability when kicking since you are standing on one foot. For this reason, a good kicker will withdraw the leg as fast as he kicks it out, reducing the time in which he is vulnerable.

- Best targets are the groin, knees, inner and outer thighs, and top of the foot (instep).

Sonic Weapons

Often overlooked is the use of sound as a weapon. Best used as a fallback or supplemental weapon, sound can deter an attacker through discomfort, or by drawing attention to the scene.

You can carry a **compressed air sound horn**. These come in sizes small enough to carry in a pocket or purse and they emit a loud piercing blast of noise that at close ranges can startle, stun, and cause pain and even injury to the ears of an attacker.

In addition, the sound can be heard up to a mile away and can attract the attention of passersby and cause the attacker to break off his attack for fear of being discovered in the act.

Another sonic device is a **rape whistle**. These can produce the same effects as the sound horn but, being lighter, they are best carried on a lanyard around the neck so that they are even more accessible.

Our final sonic weapon is the **voice**. Human vocal cords can generate a sonic burst that, can cause pain, disorientation, dizziness, and even rupture an attacker's eardrum. If being restrained in a bear hug or on the ground on your back and you are able to get your mouth close to your opponent's ear, scream directly into the ear at the same time you execute your escape technique.

Psychological Weapons

Feigned Insanity: This is an ancient tactic used to discourage attacks, or cause the attacker to underestimate you. During a sexual assault, feigning insanity can deter an attacker since many people are superstitious and/or feel uncomfortable around "crazy" people. If it does not look as if the insanity act is going to deter an attack, it can nevertheless give you the element of surprise, by suddenly transforming from a tongue-flicking nut into a focused and determined fighter.

Contagion: Calmly warn your attacker that you suffer from a rare but highly infectious incurable disease and that if any of your blood or saliva should make skin contact it will surely infect others. Few criminals will know if this is true or not, but, if someone told you they were diseased and highly infectious, would you want to take the chance the person is bluffing?

Defense Against Weapons

If an attacker openly displays a weapon, it is usually intended to intimidate the victim. If the intention was to harm or kill you, then the attacker would keep the weapon hidden until you were within effective range and then launch a surprise attack. A weapon that is displayed is an intimidation to illicit your cooperation.

As a means of self-defense, a weapon is likewise best used to intimidate and dissuade an attack. By displaying a weapon openly, you increase the perceived risk of injury to a potential attacker. An easy target is an invitation to cowardly assailants, but someone armed and therefore obviously willing to fight tooth and claw to the end, is another matter altogether.

The best defense, however, is *avoidance* – use common sense, experience, awareness, and quick thinking. However, if all else fails and you find yourself fighting an armed attacker, then the following principles may improve your chances for surviving.

Defense Against A Knife

Defending empty handed against an attacker armed with a knife requires trickery and caution.

If you have a chance to evade, delay, or distract the attacker long enough, deploy any weapon you have available to equal the odds.

If you have no weapons, use improvised weapons if you can. As discussed earlier, improvised weapons can either extend your reach or act as a shield. To extend your reach use chairs, brooms, sections of pipe or sticks, or a rolled magazine. A belt and buckle can be used as a flail. For a shield use a coat, jacket, or tablecloth wrapped around the arm to use for parrying thrusts, or use a briefcase, purse, or gym bag to block against a hacking attack. Small, hard objects, like bricks, stones, baseballs, coffee mugs and pool balls can be hurled at the attacker.

If it is not possible to obtain a weapon, you must use *extreme* caution. Either stay far out of the reach of the knife, or get extremely close to the attacker, so you can control his knife wielding arm. Keep the knife in sight at all times.

Assume a crouched position with the arms held out in front and use the forearms to deflect incoming attacks and to keep the body's vital organs, and your throat, as protected as possible. Block or parry against the attacker's forearm and elbow, stay clear of the knife. Unless you are an expert in empty hand combat, do not attempt to disarm the knife hand, at best you will lose a few fingers.

Do NOT try to kick the knife out of the hand. That shit only works in the movies. Bringing your leg up toward a blade exposes the very large femoral artery, which runs on the inner part of your legs, from your groin to just above your ankle, of your kicking leg AND of your support leg. Any martial arts school that teaches you to kick against a knife is a McDojo, garbage and you should leave it and find a school that teaches practical effective martial arts, not play-play rubbish. Yeah, I said it. Your life is too important for me, and certainly YOU, to play with.

However, kicking to the attacker's knees and shins is very effective since it does not overly expose you, and because your attacker won't expect it. A person who holds a weapon in his hand is focused on that weapon, and tends to be offensive rather than defensive. This means there is an attention deficit somewhere. Usually, they do not expect an attack anywhere else but their weapon hand. Take advantage of this inattention and attack vital targets, such as the throat, groin and knees. Wear the attacker down using evasion and tactical strikes to his blind spots. If there is an opportunity to escape and run, then do so. Only when the attacker is injured and exhausted, and you have no avenue of escape, should you attempt to disarm him.

Any attacker that uses a knife is using lethal force and your response should be just as lethal.

Defense Against A Club

The club is, thankfully, not as dangerous as the knife – no weapon is – but a strike from a club CAN kill you, so take it seriously.

Move in close. It is at arm's length that the club is most lethal.

Timing is important – you must move in hard and fast, either before the attacker has a chance to raise the club, or just after the first swing. Once you are in past the club's effective range, forget about the club since it is not a threat as long as you stay in close. The assailant will expect you to go for his weapon, so while he is preoccupied holding on to his club, take advantage of his inattention and strike the assailant directly using your most powerful short range weapons – elbows, knees, or a head-butt. If you have a knife, deploy it and then go to work.

Defense Against Flexible Weapons

Chains, belts, and whips are difficult to defend against since flexible weapons can strike around a block or parry and ensnare your arms and legs. The best strategy is to try to remain outside the effective range of the weapon until you can pick up something solid to throw at the attacker or to ensnare the weapon. For example, a bar stool with the legs held towards the attacker can ensnare the chain or flail. Alternatively, you can improvise a shield from a garbage can lid, backpack, purse, or briefcase to block while *Attacking the Corners* (see *Combat Strategies and Tactics*).

When the weapon is ensnared, the attacker's first response is to disentangle his weapon, at that moment, drop your shield and then charge your attacker, or escape. If there is no time or room to maneuver out of range, go in low and take out the attacker's legs with a tackle.

Defense Against A Gun

Defending empty hand against someone armed with a handgun is dangerous, but not impossible.

If a handgun is displayed or aimed at you from a distance of more than twenty feet, and if there is a place of safety where there are a lot of people around, then make a run for it. There are several reasons for this: first, it is unlikely that the assailant will shoot since this would attract unwanted attention, and since you saw the gun, its purpose was more to intimidate you than to kill. Even if the assailant does shoot at you, at a distance of twenty feet or more the chances of hitting a moving target is less than one in ten and the chances decrease the farther away you run. Even if you are struck by a bullet, the chances of it being a lethal wound are low, and it is far better to be wounded near possible help and rescue than to be taken away to a remote location to be robbed, raped, and then shot with no chance of crawling to safety or calling out for help.

When running, run in a zigzag pattern, which makes it much more difficult for a shooter to target you. Try to turn a corner as soon as you can and put as many obstacles between you and the attacker.

If the gun is so close that you could easily reach out and grab it, try to distract the attacker's attention and then go directly for the gun. Push the muzzle away from you – a gun's ONLY danger to you is the muzzle, the hole the bullet speeds out of – and grip it with BOTH hands.

Remember that there is always a slight delay between perception and reaction. With the aid of a distraction, this should allow enough time to grab the weapon before the assailant can aim and pull the trigger. Again, this is only possible if you are already close enough to touch the weapon. If you have to cover ground first to reach the weapon this will negate the advantage of this time gap.

Once you have gripped the weapon you must literally hang on for dear life. Use your hands to force the muzzle toward your attacker and then yank the weapon, using your body weight and arm strength, out of the attacker's hands. Once you successfully have the gun in your hands, rack the gun's slide if it is a pistol to clear any jams, bring it to your side and order the attacker to back away. If the attacker tries to fight you for the gun once you have it, you have no choice but to defend yourself.

CHAPTER TEN
COMBAT STRATEGY & TACTICS

The first rule of survival is to have a plan. Without a plan of action, confusion and panic will result. In combat, a *Strategy* is a *plan* – an outline of possible responses to a situation. *Tactics* are the methods used to implement a strategy. The following combat strategies can be applied to many situations:

Attack First

To attack first, before the opponent has readied himself for battle, has several advantages:

First, it puts the opponent on the defensive – he must react to your attacks and the slight delay in reaction works against him.

Second is the element of surprise. Surprise, in warfare, improves the odds by a factor of three meaning, using the element of surprise, one man can defeat three men; ten men can defeat thirty.

On the streets, this is called "Stealing on" someone, or catching them with a "Sucker Punch." It is one of the most often used tactics in bar room brawls and street fights. The *sucker punch* is any technique thrown without warning while your opponent's guard is down.

To guard against the sucker punch, beware of the distance between you and a potential antagonist. If he moves into your safe range, suspect an attack. Also, beware of anyone walking towards you in a direct line.

Destroy

This strategy means to use a relentless forward assault, using multiple techniques, in rapid succession. This is to overwhelm the opponent with too many areas to defend and no time to contemplate a counterattack.

Where the motivation for attack is anger, fighters often attack each other in a blind rage using a flurry of wildly swinging punches and kicks. As sloppy and unskilled as this may be, it is nevertheless difficult to avoid or defend against. If both fighters use this method, then victory will be the result of size, strength, and dumb luck.

Using this strategy with skill instead of anger is like wave after wave crashing down upon your opponent. They will eventually drown as the water overwhelms them.

Injuring the Corners

This strategy is best used when fighting a larger or more powerful opponent. The idea is to injure the attacker's hands, arms, or legs and wear him down through multiple injuries – a war of attrition.

For example, if the opponent kicks, use your elbow to crack the knee or shins of the incoming leg, or kick the knee of his support leg. If the opponent throws a punch, slam your elbow into his fist to damage his fingers, or stab his fist with a knife or the point of your key. If he reaches out to grab you, grab his fingers and dislocate them.

Evade & Counter

This is the classic guerilla strategy used when faced with a stronger enemy. When you are attacked, the enemy's greatest force is aimed directly at you. Standing your ground to fight it out would pit you against your opponent's best techniques and allow him to use the advantage of size and strength. This situation can be avoided through evasion.

Most attackers will throw only a few punches or kicks in a row. By stepping offline, moving sideways and around your opponent to avoid his strikes, uses up the attacker's time and energy until he runs out of moves or is too tired to execute them. Then, there will be a gap in his strength and awareness, when he reconsolidates his energy to launch a new attack. This is his weakest moment; this is the time to counterattack fast, hard, and viciously.

This is the strategy used by bullfighters. The Matador does not attempt to stop or kill the bull immediately; instead, he continues to evade until the bull is exhausted and near collapse. Only then does the matador approach to apply the coup de grace.

The key to applying this strategy effectively is dependent on timing. You cannot retreat or evade too quickly or too far away from your opponent or he will anticipate your movements. You must always appear within easy reach and evade the attack, as it is launched, not before. In this way, the attacker will continue to expend energy believing his next technique will finish you.

Distraction

Distraction can be applied in different ways to upset the opponent's concentration. Kick sand or dirt into his face, spit, knock over garbage cans or furniture, or yell suddenly.

The feint is also a form of distraction whereby the opponent is fooled into believing you are attacking in a certain manner and when he reacts, you change your attack to strike somewhere unexpected. For example, if you move forwards and then bring your back leg up cocked, your opponent will believe you are about to kick him and will drop his arms down to block the kick. At that moment, throw a punch at his face and he will be unable to defend in time since his guard is down.

Time And Terrain

Time and terrain both offer advantages to those who know how to use them.

To use terrain in combat is to position yourself where you have the most freedom of movement while forcing your opponent onto terrain that causes the most difficulty. It is best to fight in surroundings you are familiar with and the opponent is not. When possible, try to maneuver the opponent into a situation that puts him at a disadvantage such as on slippery ground like an ice patch or slick floor, or on tangled ground such as among tables and chairs, or tall grass and hedges. Fight with the sun at your back, and open spaces behind you. Maneuver your opponent into cramped or narrow spaces that restrict his ability to move. Take advantage of elevation, forcing the opponent to fight uphill or up thc stairs.

When possible, choose when a confrontation occurs. If the opponent is ready and willing to fight, then this is not the best time to fight. Everyone's emotional mood fluctuates, there are times when someone will be eager to do battle and other times when he wants to rest and eat. It is when the enemy's spirit is low that you should choose to fight.

Intercepting

Intercepting is an attack launched at the moment the opponent begins his attack. This requires that you anticipate the moment your opponent attacks and then attack quickly before he can complete his movement. This takes advantage of the opponent's gap in concentration. Moments before an attack is launched, the mind is frozen for an instant as it readies itself for the attack. Attacking at *that* moment catches the opponent off guard with no time to switch from attack to defense mode.

Jamming

An attack launched at the same time as the opponent's is known as *Jamming*.

This technique requires a good sense of timing, though it is not as difficult to use as intercepting.

In this case, the ideal technique would block the opponent's incoming attack while simultaneously counter-striking.

This again takes advantage of a break in the opponent's awareness, which is focused on his own attack and is unable to react quickly enough to block the counter.

Also, as the opponent moves in, he is calculating his speed and distance in order to best execute his attack; by moving in toward *him* as he moves toward *you*, you throw his timing and distancing off and he will be too slow and too close to use his intended technique.

Three Points to Remember

1. ***Breathe:*** fear and stress work to stop breathing.

2. **Relax:** start with the face and then shoulders and work down in one relaxing wave; when tense, the body is more susceptible to injury.

   Focus: head up, look at what is going on around you, and scan your surroundings with a side-to-side motion of your head.

CHAPTER ELEVEN
SURVIVING NATURAL DISASTERS

Natural disasters can occur at any time and any place. Technology provides some advance warnings of disasters such as hurricanes, tsunamis, brush fires and volcanic eruptions but with or without foreknowledge, you will only have two choices: to either evacuate and head for safety, or dig in and shelter in place. Your best chance of surviving any natural or manmade disaster is to spend a little time and money to prepare a plan, and gather some equipment and supplies.

Preparing For A Disaster

Contact your local emergency management, civil defense office, or Red Cross chapter to find out what types of disasters are most likely to occur in your area. They will be able to provide you with information on how to prepare for each.

Find out if your community has emergency

warning signals, what they sound like, and what you should do when you hear them.

If you have children attending local schools, find out about the disaster plans at your children's school or daycare center.

Make sure every family or group member has each other's contact information including telephone numbers for home, work and cell phones and e-mail addresses. Post a copy of these contact numbers somewhere in the home that even the children can find, but not where intruders in your home can readily recognize. Do NOT put your family members' or comrades' phone numbers and email addresses on the refrigerator. Intruders will look their first for valuable information on you and your cadre.

Learn the location of your home's main electric fuse box, water service main, and natural gas main. Learn how to turn these utilities off and keep an adjustable wrench nearby in case the valves are rusted or stuck.

Inspect your home for other potential hazards. Look for objects that could fall or tip over during an accident and which could cause injuries or block exits. Heavy objects such as bookshelves, dressers, and hot water heaters may need extra support or restraining straps.

During a disaster, it is important that you work with a team to increase your chances of survival. Once you have organized your home and family disaster plan, make contact with your neighbors and/or your comrades to plan how the neighborhood/cadre can work together before, during and after a disaster.

If you already belong to a neighborhood organization, such as a home association or neighborhood watch group, introduce the subject of disaster preparedness at the next meeting

Pool your talents and learn what special skills your neighbors, friends and comrades have, such as medical, technical, or emergency responder expertise. Work together to plan how to help neighbors who have special needs, such as the disabled and elderly people. Also, designate who will supervise childcare in case parents cannot get home.

Purchase and store an ABC-type fire extinguisher and instruct each family member how to use it. Be sure to test and recharge your fire extinguisher(s) according to the manufacturer's instructions.

Teach children how and when to call 911, or your local Emergency Medical Services number, for emergency help. Show each family member how and when to turn off the water, gas and electricity at the main switches.

A few simple preparations can go a long way to increasing your chances of surviving any emergency. As with all survival situations, information, knowledge and skills are more important than tools, equipment, and supplies.

Investing the relatively modest time and effort it

takes to participate in first aid courses, urban and wilderness survival weekends, and self-defense classes will pay huge dividends in increased confidence, leadership ability, and survival savvy. At the least, you should keep a first aid/home treatment manual, a wilderness survival manual, and a *Farmer's Almanac* in your home.

Disaster Plan

If you do not have a plan, your chances of survival drop. Have a family meeting and discuss why you need to prepare for disaster. Explain the possible threats unique to your environment such as wild fires, severe weather, earthquakes, floods, and the like. Discuss the types of disasters that are most likely to happen and outline a plan of action for each scenario. Plan how you will round up any young children and how you will take care of your pets.

Determine the best escape routes from your home. Plan to share responsibilities and designate specific responsibilities to each member. For example, one person will be put in charge of collecting food and water, another, the one with the most medical experience, will be in charge of monitoring medical supplies and treating injuries.

Put someone in charge of communications to ensure that everyone is accounted for, knows what the next stage in the plan is, and that outside family members and cadre are alerted to the situation. If you have school age children, designate who is in charge of picking them up.

If there are elderly or disabled people in your group, plan to secure their specific needs during a disaster. This could include special transportation, additional medicine or medical equipment, and extra assisted care. If you have pets, designate someone to ensure they have shelter, and a supply of food and water available.

Ask an out-of-state friend or family member to be your "family contact". After a disaster, it is often easier to call long distance than locally. This person would act as a Call Center where other family members who have been separated could call this person and tell them where they are, their condition, and what help they need or can offer. Make sure everyone knows this contact's phone number and address.

Rendezvous And Fallback Locations

When a disaster strikes, you and your family may be in different locations, with children at school, adults at their jobs and seniors in the home. For this reason, it is important to meet with your family and decide on two places to meet in case an emergency prevents you from returning home.

Rendezvous: The *Rendezvous* location should be close to your home and is used in emergencies that prevent you from entering your home, such as fire, a gas leak, or a crime scene investigation. Choose a place, such as the corner convenience store, or a neighbor's home, that can also provide relative safety and access to communications, food and water.

Fallback: The *Fallback* location should be outside your neighborhood and is used if you cannot return to the area because of wild fires, floods, landslides, earthquakes, or mob chaos. A close relative's home in a nearby town would be an ideal destination. Other possibilities could include a favorite hotel, resort, all night diner, cottage, or camping site. Make sure everyone in the family has a personal copy of the rendezvous and fallback addresses and phone numbers.

Bug-In Bag

The first question in a natural disaster is whether to stay or go. You need to make some simple preparations that would allow you to survive either decision. If your best choice is to stay in your home, then a few supplies set aside can ease the hardships.

A *Bug-In Bag* should provide the tools and necessities to allow you and your family to stay safe and sheltered in your home in the event that an emergency cuts you off from outside aid. It should contain food, water, and medicinal needs for everyone in your home for a minimum of three days. Supplies to include in the kit are as follows:

- *Clothing*

    Keep one full change of clothing in the bag. These should be a rugged long sleeve shirt and long pants, which offers the most protection. Choose thicker clothing if you live in colder climates.

Also essential is an extra pair of comfortable walking shoes or boots.

A pair of work gloves can come in handy when having to clean up broken glass and clear rubbish or doing emergency repairs.

Include a couple of bandanas. These can serve several functions such as head covering, dust mask, sling, sweatband, and emergency bandage.

- ### *Toiletry Kit*

Include toiletries such as soap, toothbrush and toothpaste, mirror, brush, washcloths, toilet paper, feminine products, and baby powder and diapers if there are infants in the home.

Staying clean is an important component in survival to prevent infections and diseases and to improve morale.

- ### *Maps*

Get a recent and detailed map of your area in case you have to move or find nearby streams, railroads and the like.

- ### *Money and Documents*

Keep a small amount of both cash and coins. In some emergencies, ATMs, cash machines, and credit card scanners may not function. You may need cash to purchase extra supplies or fuel for your automobile.

It is also a good idea to include copies of important family documents – birth certificates, passports and licenses – in your bag. In the event your home and/or personal possessions are destroyed, you will have a much easier time having important documents re-issued if you have copies of the originals.

Store all of the above items together in a durable backpack since you may not have time to collect all these items from separate areas of the home during a disaster. Keep the bag in an easily accessible, cool, dry, dark place, such as a storm cellar or walk-in closet.

Water

Drinkable water is an easily overlooked necessity because of its everyday availability, but in emergencies, water can quickly become a rare commodity.

The average adult will lose 2 to 3 liters of water per day during modest exertion at room temperature. Therefore, 2 to 3 liters would be the minimum requirement of fresh drinking water per adult per day. However, if you live in a hot and arid environment you could lose up to 2 to 3 liters of water per *hour*. In this type of climate, you would need to drink 14 to 30 liters of water per day.

Factors such as extreme weather, intense physical activity, injuries or illness, can cause your body to lose even more water. If you do not replace this water, you will begin to suffer dehydration. Dehydration is a serious danger in a survival situation since it decreases your efficiency and ability to think and will increase the effects of injuries and shock. You should replenish fluids even when you are not thirsty. *By the time you feel thirsty you are already 2 percent dehydrated.*

The best way to prevent dehydration is to replace fluids as you use them by drinking small amounts of water at regular intervals rather than to stop and drink a large quantity at one time.

If there is plenty of water but food is scarce, compensate by increasing your fluid intake to 6 to 8 liters of water per day. In extreme conditions of little food and much physical activity you could also suffer from a loss of electrolytes (body salts) and supplemental sources may be required. A solution of a 0.25 teaspoon of salt diluted in 1 liter of water will provide a day's worth of salt to replenish the lost electrolytes.

If there are no renewable sources for drinkable water, you may need to ration the available water until another source is found. In a survival situation, a minimum intake of a half a liter (0.5 liter) of a sugar-water mixture (2 teaspoons of sugar per liter) per day will prevent severe dehydration for a week or more, provided you limit physical activity and are protected from the extremes of climate.

Common Signs And Symptoms Of Dehydration

- Dark urine with a very strong odor

- Low urine output

- Dark, sunken eyes

- Fatigue

- Emotional instability

- Loss of skin elasticity

- Delayed capillary refill in fingernail beds (Press lightly on your fingernail so that the color becomes lighter, release and the color should almost instantly return to normal)

- Trench line down center of tongue

The escalating effects of dehydration are as follows:

- 5 percent loss of body fluids results in thirst, irritability, nausea, and weakness.

- 10 percent loss results in dizziness, headache, inability to walk, and a tingling sensation in the limbs.

- 15 percent loss results in dim vision, painful urination, swollen tongue, deafness, and a numb feeling in the skin.

- Greater than 15 percent of body fluids may result in death.

The average healthy person can live 3 to 5 days without water before expiring.

Storing Water

Storing water for long periods can be a problem. The easiest solution is to purchase pre-packaged bottled water. You can also store emergency tap water in plastic containers that can be found in most stores. Make sure that the containers are appropriate for water storage. If not, there is the risk that chemicals will penetrate the container and contaminate the water. Glass bottles are also safe, but are more difficult to store and too easily broken.

Carefully wash the container and let it completely dry before filling it. Add some chlorine bleach – about ten drops per gallon of water. This will kill most microorganisms, without having too much impact on the taste.

Fill the container completely to the top, to force out all the air.

Store the water off the floor, in a place where it cannot freeze (frozen water will expand and break the container), away from direct sunlight, and away from chemicals.

A last minute solution is to fill your bathtubs and sinks with cold water. It is best to ensure the bathtub and sinks are clean and disinfected first. In an emergency, one source for approximately four liters of water is the toilets' holding tank (The water in the tank above the bowl). *Warning:* this water MUST be treated (see below).

Water Treatment

If fresh water becomes scarce, you may have to use water from questionable sources, even water that has a bad smell and taste and may be contaminated by bacteria and parasites that cause diseases such as dysentery, cholera, typhoid, and hepatitis. In a survival situation you may need to use this water but you have to filter and treat the water first.

First, filter out any foreign materials, such as leaves or dirt, using a piece of cloth or coffee filter. Strain the water into a pot or can and bring it to a rolling boil for at least one full minute. Let the water cool for thirty minutes. This will kill any microorganism that could cause illness.

However, if you are unable to boil the water, you can resort to chemical treatments. There are two types of commonly available chemicals used to treat water - iodine and chlorine.

Iodine is sensitive to light, which is why it is always sold in a dark bottle. It works best if the water is over 68° F (21° C). *Warning:* some people are allergic to iodine – people with active thyroid disease, or pregnant women cannot use iodine as a form of water purification.

Add 5 drops of 2% tincture of Iodine per quart when the water is clear. Add 10 drops per quart when the water is cloudy.

Chlorine has long been used to disinfect water and can be used for people with iodine allergies or restrictions. The most common complaint is the chemical taste in the treated water.

Treating Water with a 5-6 Percent Liquid Chlorine Bleach Solution:

- 1 quart/1 liter: 3 drops to 5 drops

- ½ gallon/2 quarts/2 liters: 5 drops to 10 drops

- 1 gallon: 1/8 teaspoon to 1/4 teaspoon

- 5 gallons: ½ teaspoon to 1 teaspoon

After adding the chemical to the water, swish it around to help dissolve it. Splash some of the treated water onto the lid, spout, and the threads of the water bottle so that all areas are disinfected. Allow the water to sit for at least 30 minutes after adding the chemical to allow purification to occur. The colder the water, the less effective the chemical is as a purifying agent. It is best if water is at least 60° F (16° C) before treating.

You can improve the taste of the treated water by pouring it back and forth between containers, or you can add a pinch of salt per quart or add flavorings such as lemonade mix.

Halazone tablets are another convenient and inexpensive water purification method used by wilderness survivalists. However, there are two disadvantages to their use: reliable disinfection requires six tablets per liter for 1-hour of contact, resulting in a horrid taste to the water. In addition, the tablets rapidly lose effectiveness when exposed to warm, humid air.

In addition to your stored water, keep a canteen or two of clean water attached to – or inside – your Bug-In Bag.

Food

Your Bug-In Bag should also contain enough food for a minimum of three days. You must store the same amount of food for each person in your family.

Foods that require minimum preparation and have a long shelf life, such as canned, powdered or dehydrated foods, and preserves are most practical.

Be sure to include some power bars, dried fruit and snack foods, not only as portable nutrition but also as a sweet treat to improve morale.

If you have pets, you should store some pet food as well.

If the power and gas have been cut off, you will have to improvise ways of cooking. Alternative cooking sources include candle warmers, fondue pots, or a fireplace. Do not use charcoal grills and camp stoves indoors since they produce carbon monoxide and need outdoor ventilation. You can eat commercially canned food right out of the tin without heating, or you can heat the contents in the can itself. Just remove the label, wash and disinfect the can, and then open the can before heating it.

Although you can live 3 to 6 weeks without food, you need a certain minimum amount of calories to function. Without food, your mental and physical capabilities will deteriorate rapidly, and you will become weak and unfocused.

The average person needs 2,000 calories per day to function at a minimum level. In extreme weather conditions and vigorous activity such as hiking through the wilderness, you may require up to 6,000 calories per day to prevent starving.

An inadequate caloric intake will lead to starvation and then your body will feed on its own tissue for energy. Food also provides vitamins, minerals, salts, and other elements essential to good health. Possibly more important, it helps morale.

First Aid Kit

Ideally, you should have a commercial grade first aid kit in your Bug-In Bag that is large enough to care for all the members in your household.

Quality store bought kits are adequate but you should add other items to it, such as medical and prescription needs. If you require daily medication, keep a minimum three-day supply in your kits. Keep these in the original bottles with the doctor and pharmacy information on the label. If you require glasses, an extra pair of prescription glasses should also be included. Other items you might want to include that are not normally found in first aid kits are:

- Multivitamins, and natural antibiotics such as Tea Tree Oil, Grape Seed Extract and Golden Seal.

- Antibiotics. If you have been prescribed an antibiotic for a previous infection, ask for a second refill and then store these for emergency use only.

- Prescription pain killer – for serious injuries, over-the-counter pain relievers will be inadequate.

- Water purification tablets.

- Magnifying glass – to see and remove glass shards and slivers.

- Dental cement – great for emergency fixes involving broken teeth or fillings.

- Suture Kit, for immediate life threatening wounds.

- Surgical scalpel.

- Potassium iodide, to treat radiation sickness.

- Baking soda, used for chemical and radiation decontamination.

- Clip-on mini flashlight, for treating injuries at night.

- A comprehensive first aid manual.

Also, be sure to complete a standard first aid and CPR course. There is no excuse for not learning such essential survival and life-saving skills.

Tools And Equipment

In addition to the food, water and medicine, you should also store some equipment that may be useful in an emergency. These include:

- Flashlight and extra batteries

- Portable radio, to monitor weather and public service broadcasts. A multi-band, emergency, hand rechargeable radio is best

- Safety candles or an oil burning storm lantern (oil lamps can be run on cooking oil)

- Propane camping style cooking stove

- One or more coolers. Inexpensive Styrofoam coolers will work just as well. These can be used to refrigerate perishable food items after a power outage for several hours

- A multi-tool – handy for opening cans and bottles and small emergency repairs

- A crowbar, used for opening doors and windows that have become wedged in their frames, breaking locks and chains, or digging an escape hole through a wall or roof

- Dust mask, plastic sheeting and duct tape to make emergency repairs and to cover doors and windows in case of bio/chemical disasters

- Decontamination supplies, including soap, water, bleach, and baking soda

- Packaged moist towelettes, garbage bags and plastic ties

- An adjustable wrench or pliers to turn off water and or gas valves

- Pencil and paper, to leave behind notes to family or comrades if you need to evacuate

- Deck of cards, and a few books to pass the time

Bug-Out Bag

Several types of disasters such as floods, wildfires, or earthquakes may require you to evacuate the area quickly and seek shelter elsewhere. A *Bug-Out Bag* ("BOB") contains the supplies you need to survive for 72 hours while traveling. This bag should be prepared in advance since time may be of the essence.

A good BOB must contain items that you are familiar with, and know how to use. If you put the bag together yourself you will know what is in it, why it's there and how to use it. Buying an off-the-shelf BOB or 72-Hour Kit might be simple, less time consuming, and maybe even less expensive – until you really need it. During a crisis is NOT the time to discover that all you really have is a fancy bag filled with mostly impractical stuff that you are not familiar with and cannot use. Make your own Bug-Out Bag; you will not regret it.

A good BOB should contain what you need and nothing more. Weight and space limitations will determine how much you can realistically carry. It is one thing to throw a bag into a vehicle; it is quite another to have to carry that bag yourself. Most people tend to underestimate just how difficult it is to carry a lot of weight over long distances. If you have any doubts, give it a test run one weekend and see how it goes. My guess is that after a few miles, you will have a very different notion of what is – and what is NOT – going in your bag.

For the bag itself, get a sturdy backpack with

heavy-duty padded straps. Try to avoid the military/tactical looking bags since these will draw unwelcome attention to you and possibly invite trouble.

The contents lists below are tailored to the various levels of crises you might find yourself dealing with. If all you can afford right now are the *Code Yellow* contents, that is fine, but you want to cover all levels as soon as possible. You never know what kind of crisis might occur.

The *Urban Survival and Preparedness Institute* has packages by code, as well as individual items, for sale at the most reasonable prices. You can reach us at USPIpacks@gmail.com.

Code Yellow

Code Yellow means there is no specific threat but you are aware of some crisis that may be on the horizon. *Example:* A potential hurricane or snow storm. The people trapped on the expressway for two days, by 1" of snow, in Atlanta were in Code Yellow (even though they THOUGHT they were in Code Red)

Be sure to have the following items in your bag:

- Cell Phone
- Hat with a flexible brim
- Cotton bandana
- Shemagh (head/neck scarf)
- Sunglasses (safety)
- Rain poncho
- Trash bags

- Band Aids
- Elastic bandages
- Gauze pads
- Insect repellant
- Mylar Survival Blanket
- Popsicle sticks
- Rubbing alcohol (packs and bottle)
- Surgical tape
- Triple Antibiotic Ointment / Golden Seal
- Survival knife
- Multi-Tool
- LED headlamp
- Mini LED keychain
- Emergency whistle

Code Orange

Code Orange means there is a specific threat serious enough for us to have gassed up all the vehicles and be prepared to bug-out. The cause for a Code Orange is terrorist threats, economic uncertainty, looming war, severe weather (tornadoes; hurricanes; floods; blizzards) political unrest, etc. *Example:* The beginning of Hurricane Katrina was Code Orange; the Ferguson uprising was Code Orange.

Add these items to the bag you already have for Code Yellow:

- Drinking water (3 Liters)
- Collapsible water bottle
- Hard water bottle
- Metal water bottle / canteen
- Protein energy bars (Qty 6)

- Ignition source (Qty 3) (matches; lighters; battery; etc.)
- Tinder (Qty 3) (lint; cotton balls coated in petroleum jelly; steel wool; etc.)
- Machete
- Map of the area
- Compass
- Pepper spray
- Handgun
- Multi-Tool
- 550 parachute cord (50')
- Extra batteries for flashlights
- $100 cash
- Toilet paper

Code Red

This is the most severe of Codes. *Code Red* means the event that triggered a Code Orange has affected our immediate area or has national implications. Events such as a terrorist attack on a major city, riots, a sudden collapse of the Market, an outbreak of a regional conflict in the Middle East and a viral pandemic are classified as major, non-weather, events with devastating impact.

Add these items to your bag:

- Tarp
- Tent
- Sleeping bag
- Ground pad
- Wool blanket
- Protein / energy bars (Qty 6)

- MREs / dehydrated meals (Qty 3)
- Spork
- P-38 can opener
- Metal cooking pot
- Metal cup
- Pot scrubber
- Portable stove
- Stove fuel (Qty 8 Tablets)
- Lightweight long sleeve shirt
- Convertible (zip-off) pants
- Underwear
- Wool hiking socks (Qty 3 pair)
- Medium weight fleece
- Working gloves
- 12-gauge shotgun (20-gauge, or .410 bore shotgun for children and smaller women)
- Rifle (sniper, hunting, or assault; the choice is yours)
- Ammunition (minimum 25 rounds per firearm)
- Duct tape (25')
- 55 gal. contractor garbage bag (Qty 2)
- Resealable bags (Qty 5, various sizes)
- N95 sunglasses
- Face mask
- Sewing kit
- Latex tubing (3')
- Fishing kit
- Condoms (non-lubricated)
- Binoculars (optional)
- Face paint
- Light glowstick

- Mini LED light
- Candles
- Batteries
- Crank power charger
- Emergency radio with hand crank
- Water filters / purification systems
- Water purification tablets (Qty 3)

Keep it Current

Go through your BOB at least once every three months and keep it up to date and relevant. Take out all the contents, inspect their condition and then repack it. Always pack your bag in the order in which you expect you might need the contents. For obvious reasons, you would never bury your extra ammunition magazines down at the very bottom of the BOB.

Also, if you are forced to leave your location, you do not want to empty the entire contents of your BOB for all to see, searching for an item way down at the bottom. The contents you expect to need first should be at the very top. And do NOT store your entire stash of anything in one location in your bag. For example, keep your money in several different pockets. If you must take out cash to pay for something you do not want to pull out a large amount of cash in front of strangers.

Finally, keep your BOB in a secure location, away from prying eyes and children, but handy enough that you would be able to grab it and go without delays or complications. Do not ever raid your BOB for anything you do not intend to replace *immediately.*

Adjust your supplies as the seasons change, and make sure to periodically rotate your contents and freshen up your food supplies, water, batteries, etc.

Ideally, you should have one backpack prepared for each person in the household. Each Bug-Out Bag should contain all the items needed for one person for three days. In other words, do not put all the water and food into one pack and all the tools in another. This redundancy is intentional since in the event that you should become separated, each person will be self-sufficient and have an equal chance of survival. Alternatively, if one of the packs is lost or destroyed, you will still have all the tools necessary in the remaining pack or packs. In addition, this allows you to replace items that become lost or broken, which helps ensure that you will always have the minimum of tools required to survive.

What To Do During A Disaster

If disaster strikes, remain calm. Remember to breathe, relax, and take things one at a time. Put your plan into action. If there is much confusion among your group, be prepared to take a leadership role. Someone with some disaster knowledge taking charge is better than a disorganized mob.

First, check to see if there are any immediate threats or hazards such as fire, gas or chemical leaks, rising floodwaters, structural instability and impending collapse.

Next, determine whether it is safer to stay where you are, or to move. Generally, in disasters such as wild fires, floods, and hurricanes, shelter is sought by moving out of the path of destruction. In disasters such as tornados, ice storms, power outages, and pandemics, the best recourse is to stay put.

Threats from earthquakes are more difficult to assess since much depends on the structural integrity, and the possibility of wild fires. If the building you are in seems intact and stable and there are no signs of fire, then it is best to stay where you are. However, if the building appears to have been damaged by the quake, and/or there are fires breaking out, then you must bug-out since there is a risk that aftershocks may further weaken and collapse the structure.

If You Stay

If there are no immediate dangers that necessitate evacuation, the next course of action is to see to the health and safety of your family or group members.

In cases where schools institute procedures to shelter-in-place, you may not be permitted to drive to the school to pick up your children. Even if you go to the school, the doors will likely be locked "to keep your children safe." Consider carrying a good set of bolt cutters. That is all I will say in regard to that. Monitor local media outlets for announcements about changes in school openings and closings.

Do a head count to ensure no one is missing. If someone in your family or party is missing, send the ablest member of your group to do a search within 50 yards of your home. You do not want that person to search too far since they may also risk becoming lost. If anyone that is missing is further away, then you may have to organize and equip a Search and Rescue team with your remaining group members (See *Search & Rescue*, below).

Check for injuries. If you several people have multiple injuries, you will need to set up a triage system. Identify the most serious injuries first, such as stopped breathing, no pulse, and severe bleeding. Make sure that these people get help first and are evacuated to medical facilities as soon as possible. If you are unable to evacuate the injured to emergency services you will need to set up a treatment area and apply first aid yourself until medical help arrives.

Change into rugged clothing with long sleeves and long pants for extra protection and wear sturdy shoes. These should be a part of your Bug-In AND Bug-Out Bags. Be sure to wear garden or work gloves when searching through rubble.

Call any family members that were away from home when the disaster struck and then call your Family Contact. Provide him or her with information on your situation and what type of help you may need.

Check on your neighbors, especially the elderly or disabled. Confine or secure your pets. Animals easily panic and can do injury to themselves and others.

Secure your home and immediate area by checking for dangers and hazards. Clean up and remove broken glass and furniture, check on the building's structural stability, secure heavy objects from tipping over, and watch for smoldering fires.

Sniff for gas leaks, starting at the water heater. If you smell gas or suspect a leak, turn off the main gas valve, open windows, and get everyone outside quickly. Use only flashlights until the area is safe. Do NOT turn on electrical switches, light matches or use any open flame such as candles or gas lamps.

Use your telephone (cellular or landlines) only for emergencies.

Also, do not drive or go out of your home unless absolutely necessary.

If power has been cut, listen to your battery-powered radio for news and weather reports.

Once any immediate threats have been addressed and there is no need to evacuate, then resume as many of your normal daily routines as possible. This is especially important if there are young children in your home to help alleviate their fears and anxiety.

If You Go

Keep a full tank of gas in your car if you can. At a minimum, keep half a tank at *all times*. Gas stations will most likely be closed during emergencies and you will not be able to pump gas during power outages.

Plan to take one car per family to reduce congestion and delay. If you do not own a car, make transportation arrangements with friends and comrades.

Before you leave your home, shut off water and electricity, if you have time. However, leave the natural gas service on unless you smell gas. Once turned off, only a utility representative can restore gas service to your home. You may need gas for heating and cooking when you return, and in the aftermath of a disaster, it could take weeks for a professional to respond.

Call your Family Contact to report where you are going, what route you are taking, and when you expect to arrive. Close and lock the doors and windows and draw the blinds and curtains. Post a note in a non-obvious, previously designated area, telling others when you left and where you are going.

Take your Bug-Out Bag. Be sure to bring your photo identification because the authorities may not allow people to re-enter a disaster area without identification.

Take your pets with you - do not leave them behind. Pets are usually not allowed in public shelters, so you should go to a relative or friend's home, or find a "pet-friendly" hotel. If there are no other alternatives, you may have to house your pets outside the shelter or in your vehicle in their carrying boxes and ensure they have adequate water and food. Check in on them regularly.

If you live in a big city and the city is being evacuated, then the roads out will be hopelessly gridlocked within *minutes* and you will get nowhere. Take side streets and back roads. If however, there is flooding or wildfires, then taking those same shortcuts could lead you right into the disaster.

Bugging-In is usually the better option during a disaster. If you *must* bug-out, traveling on foot is a safer option than trying to drive.

Start taking hikes, working your way up to jogging and maneuvering through obstacle courses. If you are out of shape when a disaster strikes, it could cost your life or the lives of your loved ones.

Aftermath

The effects of a disaster can also have devastating emotional impact on survivors. The loss of personal property, loved ones, and pets can cause shock, disbelief, grief, anger and guilt. Memory problems, anxiety and/or depression are also possible after experiencing a disaster. Those especially at risk are children, senior citizens, and people with disabilities.

Children are more likely to become afraid and so it is important to make them feel they are safe. Seniors are more likely to experience disorientation, and the disabled are more likely to worry about having access to their medications and other special needs. In all such instances, speak calmly and assure everyone that they will have a safe place to stay, and that all their needs will be provided for.

Things you can do to improve morale include:

- Make sure everyone has plenty of food, drinks and rest. Some sweets or other treats are a positive sign that things will be back to normal soon.

- Try to return to as many of your personal and family routines as possible. Do some things together that everyone can enjoy, such as playing some sports, or playing a board game.

- Stay positive and limit the amount of sensational and negative news coverage your family is exposed to. If you go back to inspect a damaged home, leave your children with family or friends. The impact of seeing the destruction will add to their fears.

Also, take extra care with your pets. Animals can become upset and panicked and may scratch, bite or otherwise act aggressively after a disaster. Comfort them by speaking in a calm voice, and ensure they have food, water, and treats, if available. Try to find an old blanket or toy they had to reassure them. Keep your pets secured during and after a disaster since they may injure themselves if they are loose to wander into a disaster area.

Search_&_Rescue

During a natural or manmade disaster people can become separated from their families and communities and go missing. One of the first post-disaster activities is to find, and care for, those that are lost.

Some knowledge of *Search and Rescue* (SAR) methods can be useful in locating missing family members before, during, or after a disaster.

Search and Rescue operations typically have three distinct phases"

1. Assessment and Assembly Phase

Gather your family or group, discuss the situation, and collect information about the missing person, such as:

- Age

- Gender

- Physical description; what clothes they were wearing

- Last known location and their intended destination

- How physically fit they are; what equipment or modes of transportation they use.

  If you are searching for someone that is young, physically fit, and those carrying survival equipment, you may have to search a wider area since they are more likely to cover greater distances than children, the elderly, or anyone that is injured.

Based on the information gathered, make a list of possible locations to search. For example, in searching for lost children a list of possible locations would include local schools, playgrounds, friends' homes, malls and so on.

Study an area map and review likely travel routes, such as streets, foot or bicycle paths, parks, ravines, trails, and streams. The missing party's personal interests may offer clues; children will tend to head for their schools, teenagers to a park, mall, or cafe.

Decide who will form part of the rescue team and who will stay at home or base camp. You always need one person to stay at base camp to handle communications and in case the lost party returns.

Prepare some rescue equipment, which should include communications such as walkie-talkies, or cell phones if service is available, first aid kit, maps and compass and/or global positioning system (GPS) unit, food and water, simple shelter making materials, and signal flares.

2. Search Phase

The first rule of searching is: do not make the situation worse by getting lost or injured *yourself.* Make sure that conditions are safe enough to go out in. Incoming storms, hurricanes, floods, chemical spills, and wildfires may make it too dangerous to mount a search at that time.

Form a *Fast Team* – a few members that travel light, move fast and search just the most likely locations. For example, a lost child could theoretically be anywhere within several square miles from your home, but to do a grid search, checking every square meter of ground would be slow, and requires lots of manpower. It would also not make much sense. A Fast Team would search just those areas and routes deemed the most likely locations the child would be, such as the basketball court or her grandma's house.

The team is given specific targets to search, a timetable so that home base knows when to expect them back, and specific routes to take.

Along the route, searchers should call out for the victim, look for tracks, question potential witnesses, and search for any other clues such as an abandoned vehicle, clothing, and supplies, or campsites. If, after searching those targets, the missing person is not found, the team should return to home base for debriefing.

3. *Rescue* Phase

If you find the missing person, first do an examination for injuries. If they are conscious, question them on any injuries or pains they may have, and perform an examination of those areas. If time permits, provide first aid to any minor injuries and evacuate the person back to home base.

If there are serious injuries, call or signal other rescuers to the scene. Keep the victim warm and off the ground if possible. Warm up a hypothermic person immediately with extra clothing, hot drinks, a fire and close contact with another person.

If the person is unconscious, check for breathing. If he or she is not breathing, tilt their head back, clear the airway in their throat of any obstructions, and begin mouth-to-mouth respiration and/or CPR. If a neck or back injury is suspected, move the victim only if he or she is in immediate danger or if emergency responders with a good amount of first aid or paramedic skill and experience cannot be brought to the site. Consult a comprehensive first aid manual for further information on how to safely transport a severely injured victim.

USAR

Urban Search and Rescue (USAR) is the term used to describe the location, extrication, and initial medical stabilization of victims trapped in confined spaces, usually from structural collapse, due to major disasters.

In cases of disasters in urban environments that involve widespread structural damage, search and rescue efforts become more hazardous. In the event that professionals are unavailable and you have to search for lost friends and family after such a disaster, the following describes some essential procedures:

Assessment Stage

Instead of determining likely locations for a person lost in a geographical area, USAR assessment tries to determine likely locations of survivors in a structure. Gather information on the types of structures involved, the extent of damage, the layout of the building involved, and what hazards are present, such as downed power lines, natural gas leaks, flooding, animals, hazardous materials, or unstable structures. Structural damage can be categorized as light, moderate, or heavy.

In addition to walkie-talkies, cell phones, a first aid kit, food and water, USAR equipment, should include:

- Construction boots with steel toes and steel sole inserts to protect against stepping on exposed nails and broken glass

- Hardhat with headlight – improvise by using a bicycle or rock climbing helmet and strap on a flashlight

- Safety glasses – the type used in workshops; or improvise and use ski goggles to protect against dust and hazards such as fiberglass.

- Dust mask – many building materials are toxic if breathed in as dust

- Leather work gloves and knee pads, for protection when crawling or digging through rubble

- Crowbar, axe, or hatchet, for chopping through debris and leveraging open jammed doors and windows

- Car-jack or hand winch – can be used to lift and pull away heavy obstructions

Search

Scarchers should work in pairs known using a method called *Two-in, Two-out*. The principle of *Two-in, Two-out* mandates that rescuers never go into a dangerous situation alone. There should always be at least two rescuers that go together when they enter a location and at least two when they come out. In addition, two additional rescuers should remain outside the building, ready with rescue tools, in order to provide backup rescue if the team inside becomes endangered.

While you search, call out for victims to try to identify their location. Searchers should stop frequently to listen for noises or attempted communication from victims; often this involves all searchers stopping activity at the same time to listen.

Search using a systematic search pattern such as a *right/left* search pattern – one team searches the left side and one team the right side of a building; or a *bottom-up/top-down* search pattern.

Possible locations of victims inside damaged structures include the spaces that are found between collapsed floors, and the lean-to space created when a single wall or floor has collapsed diagonally against another wall. Other possible locations include spaces where victims may have entered for shelter during a disaster, such as under desks or in bathtubs, closets, basements and crawlspaces.

To avoid duplication of search efforts in situations where multiple structures are searched, such as after a hurricane or earthquake, the outside of buildings are marked to indicate buildings that have already been searched. In the United States, markings on the fronts of structures are standardized as follows:

- A *single diagonal slash*: a search in the building is in progress.

- An *X inside a three-foot square*: "Dangerous! Do Not Enter!"

- *An X with writing around it:* means the search is completed. The writing around the X tells you the following information:

  - Time and date the search was completed is written *above the X*

- Search Team's identifier is written to *the left of the X*

- Results of the search (i.e. number of victims or rescued) is written *below the X*

- Any additional hazards, such as gas leaks, structural damage, or animals is written *to the right of the X*

- Marks are made with cans of spray paint, usually in Day-Glo orange.

Rescue

When you find a victim, first check them for injuries and then administer first aid on site if possible. Before removing the victim you may first have to remove and/or stabilize surrounding debris. This can be accomplished by using leverage to lift heavy objects, or by constructing a rectangular wooden framework known as a box crib underneath the object to be stabilized. Leveraging and cribbing can be combined.

Victims who cannot walk out on their own can be removed using lifts, drags, or carries. Remove victims carefully to avoid any further injury. Where any neck or back injury is suspected, the spine should be immobilized first before attempting to move them. Also, avoid dragging injured victims where the presence of debris and broken glass would cause further injury.

What To Do If YOU Are Lost

During a disaster or when evacuating, it is easy for you or members of your family or group to become separated and lost. Make sure everyone learns the following basic strategies to use if they should become separated from the main group and are lost:

- First, once you realize you are lost, *stop, stay calm, and assess your situation.*

  Do not continue to wander around. Look around to make sure you are in an area that does not pose an immediate danger – you do not want to be in the path of an avalanche, near a flooding river, or in the path of a wildfire.

- If you are in a group, do not split up. Finding a group is easier than looking for scattered individuals. In addition, a group can pool resources and offer moral support.

- If you are in a safe location, hunker down and do an equipment check. Note what you or your group are carrying that would assist in a survival situation. This includes food and water, shelter materials, communications, maps and compasses, and survival tools. Your next decision is whether to stay put, or to try to find your way out.

When To Stay Put

It is best to make camp and stay put if any of the following conditions exist:

- When it gets dark. You should ideally stop moving at least two hours before sunset so that you still have enough sunlight to make camp and gather firewood. Moving at night in rough or unfamiliar terrain is a recipe for disaster.

- If you are exhausted, sick or injured. Exhaustion and injury will affect your judgment, increasing your chances of further accidents in addition to worsening pre-existing injuries.

- During extreme weather. In addition to the hazards from slippery terrain, reduced visibility, and risk of falling tree branches, your food and water requirements increase dramatically. If there are children in your party, moving can increase the possibility of separation.

Find or build a shelter that will protect you from wind and precipitation.

Stay near manmade landmarks, such as trails, power or railway lines, roads, or dams. These areas are usually searched first.

If it is safe to do so, and you have the tools to do so, build a fire. In addition to warmth and psychological comfort, a fire is visible from a great distance at night and search dogs may be able to lock on the smoke trail and find your camp.

Make your location visible by hanging brightly colored strips of cloth, plastic or paper from surrounding tree branches. If in alpine conditions, set your skis out in a cross, lay out colored ground sheets or excess clothing on the snow.

If you have a whistle, or can generate a loud whistle with your lips, then whistle several times an hour. At night, if you have a flashlight, you can shine the flashlight while turning in a circle a few times an hour. After each light or whistle signal, pause, listen, and look for any return signals from search parties. Groups of three are the universal distress signal. Three fires, three flickers from a flashlight, three blasts on a whistle, three gunshots from a hunting rifle.

If conditions improve and/or you have rested through the night, then reassess the situation. If there is no sign of rescuers, and if you have a good idea where you are and where you can find safety you may decide to try to find your way.

When To Try To Find Your Way

Finding your own way is an option provided that:

- You have plenty of daylight.

- You have a good idea of your location.

- You know which direction you need to head toward.

- You know how much ground you need to cover, and no one is injured.

Trying to walk out on your own may also be the *only* option under the following conditions:

- If the temperature drops suddenly and you do not have additional clothes or shelter materials, you may need to keep moving to avoid hypothermia.

- If you did not leave your travel plans with anyone and you are certain that no one will report you missing for several days or weeks. In this case, no search parties will be looking for you, so you must try to find safety on your own.

Points to keep in mind when you try to find your way:

- Pace yourself and move with caution; you do not want to make the situation worse by becoming injured as well.

- Try to follow marked trails, railways and power lines.

- As a rule, always travel down*hill*, until you find a river or stream, and then travel down*stream*. Keep following larger branches of the stream or river.

- Climb a tree or hill to gain a broader view of your area and look for a possible route to travel by.

To avoid walking in circles, choose a landmark in the distance and direction you want to travel such as a tree or rock outcropping and walk towards that landmark. When you arrive at that landmark, choose another to follow from there.

While moving, stop every hour and use your whistle to signal for possible help. Remember to stop two hours before sunset if you still have not found safety and get ready to make camp again.

Pandemics And Plagues

A pandemic is an epidemic of infectious disease that is spread through human populations across a large region such as a continent, or even worldwide.

Infectious diseases are caused by the presence of pathogenic microbial agents, including viruses, bacteria, fungi, protozoa, multi-cellular parasites, and aberrant proteins known as prions. Most of these are qualified as contagious diseases (also called communicable diseases) due to their potential of transmission from one person or species to another.

Throughout history, there have been a number of pandemics, such as the bubonic plague, smallpox and tuberculosis. Historically, pandemics occur about every 10 to 40 years, so it is likely that everyone will experience a pandemic at least once in their lifetime.

There are two types of pathogenic agents that are the cause of most epidemics; bacterial and viral. Epidemic diseases caused by pathogenic bacteria include typhoid, tuberculosis, bubonic plague, and cholera. The primary medical treatment used to combat bacterial infections are antibiotics.

Epidemic diseases caused by pathogenic viruses include smallpox, mumps, measles and a host of influenza type diseases such as Spanish flu, yellow fever, swine flu, and avian flu. The primary medical treatments used to combat viruses are vaccines.

These diseases are spread from person to person through coughing or sneezing, by touching infected surfaces, or through contamination of food or water. Most healthy adults can pass the disease to someone else before knowing they are sick, since we become infectious one day before symptoms develop and up to five days after becoming sick.

Prevention

If you have any forewarning of an impending pandemic, increase your Bug-In Bag stores from the minimum three days' worth of food and water, to three months' worth. This will help you to reduce your public exposure time by not having to go out shopping and in case local stores run out of food. Also, add to your medical kit in the event you have to treat sick family members at home.

Most hospitals and medical facilities will be overwhelmed in the first few hours of a serious pandemic. If you or anyone in your family becomes sick, your best option will likely be to nurse them at home.

If an epidemic or pandemic is reported in your area, take the following steps to help prevent the spread of the infection:

- **Social Distancing**

    Quarantine yourself voluntarily if your family members have flu symptoms to avoid infecting others.

    Encourage co-workers to stay home if they have the first signs of illness and ask them to remain at home if they have sick family members.

    Remove your children from school and day care. Reduce their contact with other children and avoid social activities.

    Avoid public gatherings and cancel any planned meetings, travel, or social events until the pandemic has burned out.

- **Hygiene**

    Wash your hands. Infectious diseases are spread by the hands more than by any other means. Any surface that has been touched by someone infected could contain the germs or virus that can be transferred to the next person who touches that same surface. Likely sources for germs are door handles, stair rails, elevator buttons and ATM machine buttons.

After touching a doorknob or handle, you should definitely wash your hands. If you have just washed your hands in a restroom and then you touch a door handle on the way out you may have put the disease right back on your hands. Use a piece of tissue paper to turn the door handle to exit.

Just having the germs or virus on your hands will not infect you. It is when you use your hands to handle food or when you touch your eyes, nose and mouth that the contagion can enter your system. Always wash your hands when handling food and avoid touching your face until after you have washed your hands. It is always a good idea to wash your hands several times a day, especially whenever you have returned from being in a public place.

- ***Wear a Mask***

If you have to go out in populated areas during a pandemic, wear a surgical or dust mask; it can help prevent infection. These style masks will have gaps usually around the nose where airborne pathogens can still easily enter, so this method is not foolproof.

Furthermore, some viruses are so small that they can pass through these filters. In addition, you need to change these masks regularly so that contamination does not build up on the mask itself.

- **Health**

   Another strategy to prevent becoming infected in a pandemic is to strengthen your immune system.

   Take plenty of vitamin C and vitamin D every day, even if you are not feeling sick.

   Eating healthy foods and exercising are the two tried and proven methods of staying healthy.

   Also, do not allow yourself to become too stressed out. Stress has been proven to reduce your body's immunity and make you more susceptible to disease. Living through a pandemic can be a stressful experience. Be sure to take time to relax and find something enjoyable for you and your family to do to reduce stress and anxiety.

   Building up your defenses will help your immune system to be as strong as possible so that if you ever do come down with the disease, your body has a better chance of fighting it.

Symptoms Of Seasonal Or Common Flu

- Loss of appetite – lackadaisical approach to eating.

- Fever. Childhood flu fevers are often more severe, but it is not uncommon for adults to run a fever in the 100s when they have the flu.

  Often a low fever – and the weakness and chills it causes – are your first hint that the flu is about to hit you full force.

- Congestion that turns into a runny nose.

- Sore throat.

- Cough that turns productive.

- Exhaustion and weakness.

- Muscle aches and pains.

All of these symptoms will tend to hit you at the same time. To overcome and treat the flu, here are natural flu remedies for your fast recovery:

- *Fluids:* You must replenish your lost fluids in order to provide your body with the strength to get rid of the flu. Drink plenty of water. Orange juice is good for its vitamin C content.

- *Sleep:* Sleep is essential to health and the body's immune system. Make sure you get plenty of it.

- *Food:* Even though you may have a lack of appetite, you need to eat and maintain a healthy nutrition to keep your body strong.

- *Rest:* Even if you do not feel like sleeping, it is far better to stay in bed and recuperate through relaxation than it is to try to go to work.

Toddlers should be seen by a pediatrician if a fever continues longer than two days and is accompanied by significant fatigue or any kind of pain

As an adult, if your fever exceeds 103 degrees, or if you have had a fever for more than three days, then you should call your doctor.

Vaccines

Generally, vaccines are the most pushed "protection" against contracting the flu. In the event of a pandemic, local medical services and churches will distribute vaccines and news and radio stations will broadcast information on where you can be vaccinated.

However, any virus that can reach pandemic proportions is going to be quite a bit different genetically from current strains of influenza, which means that existing vaccines are not likely to help. It typically takes a minimum of six months to develop and manufacture a new vaccine.

Furthermore, vaccines cause significant side effects that are usually worse than actually contracting the disease itself.

As with any emergency, the better informed you are the better you are able to make decisions that will improve your chances of survival. If there is a pandemic, do some research on the nature and severity of the contagion and do not rely only on media reports.

Antibiotics

Antibiotics are generally used to treat diseases caused by bacterial infections. However, certain bacteria are evolving resistance to current antibiotics. A resistant strain of any of the bacterial diseases could result in a serious pandemic that may be more difficult or even impossible to treat with current antibiotics.

Furthermore, if the cause of the pandemic is bacteriological then by the very fact that it is a pandemic, suggests that the strain is already immune to existing antibiotics hence its rapid spread.

There have also been reports of healthy patients developing an autoimmune response known as a *cytokine storm*, in response to some forms of the flu. For those who are concerned about an autoimmune response to the flu, many health experts are saying that taking plenty of vitamin A can help avoid that.

Aftermath

Should the pandemic continue and its effects worsen, you may see a breakdown in social services.

First, essential services such as fire, ambulance, hospital and medical clinics will be overwhelmed. With many people ill and many more afraid to go to work, there may not be enough people to run the machinery of a city. Services, such as water, power, and transportation may decline or even cease. Retail food, convenience, and grocery stores may close due to lack of deliveries or out of fear of infection by its workers. Most likely, schools, daycares, and universities will close temporarily in order to halt the spread of the infection. Implementing social distancing will result in most social events being cancelled.

Your best option is to stay sheltered at home.

A pandemic may come in waves, each of which can last for six to eight weeks. This may continue for up to 18 months. Make sure that you have a Bug-In Bag and follow the procedures for sheltering in place.

CHAPTER TWELVE
SURVIVING SOCIAL DISASTERS

The modern urban environment will periodically experience varying degrees of social disorder during which normally available services, such as fire and ambulance departments, are unable to respond to emergencies. These events include blackouts, riots, martial law, terrorist attacks and varying degrees of warfare.

During such an event, you may have to fend for yourself for a few days or weeks until the situation returns to normal. Following the previous disaster preparedness guidelines should be sufficient to enable you and your family to survive. However, a few extra precautions may be in order:

Extra precaution against home invasion should be instituted. Secure your home and ensure that doors and windows are locked and curtains drawn. If your home has not been previously secured with entry-proof devices, you may need to reinforce possible entry points by sliding a cabinet against a window or wedging a chair under the door handle.

Move your *Bug-In Bag* into the *Safe Room* and have everyone sleep in the Safe Room at night, even if that means mattresses on the floor. If your home is vandalized or robbed, you do not want family members caught in different rooms of the house.

Check and ready any commercial weapons you have such as pepper spray, a combat slingshot, or firearms. If you do not have any commercial weapons, remember you can improvise using household objects such as a baseball bat, a can of aerosol spray, or a heavy sock filled with quarters.

Keep candles, lamps or lights low at night. Do not play the television or radio too loudly – you do not want to advertise your presence. Stay indoors and avoid unnecessary travel.

Monitor television and/or the internet if available. If these are unavailable, you should have an emergency battery – or hand cranked – radio to monitor news and emergency broadcasts.

Blackouts

Sudden power outages often accompany storms and natural disasters and can result from system malfunctions. The following steps will help ensure your safety:

Get your flashlight and find the other members of your family or group. Make sure everyone is uninjured and accounted for.

Next, turn off all electrical appliances such as electric stoves or ovens, electric blankets, eclectic space heaters, and air conditioners. The sudden power surge created by having all these appliances on at the moment the power returns can blow a fuse or even create a fire hazard.

Next, go outside or look out your window and check to see if anyone else still has their lights on, or in daytime you can check with neighbors to see if they still have power. This way you can determine if your home's main fuse has blown, or if there is a local or district wide blackout.

Gather candles, blankets, if needed, and family together and listen to your battery-powered emergency radio for news and weather reports.

Emergency Lighting

An emergency light is a battery-backed lighting device that comes on automatically when a building experiences a power outage. Emergency lights are standard in new commercial buildings. There are also residential versions that you can purchase and easily install in your home.

At the very least, you need a supply of candles. Ordinary candles are fine, but long-burning candles are recommended. Remember to include some waterproof matches and/or a few cigarette lighters. Also, keep a couple of extra flashlights – battery operated, windup or solar powered.

Portable Generators

In the event of a power failure, a portable generator can help restore some semblance of normality, which can ease nerves during an emergency when the power is shut off for an extended time.

A portable generator only really needs to power the refrigerator, a few lights, and a radio. Appliances are plugged directly into the generator's power outlets using an extension cord.

Keep in mind that the use of a generator is a short-term solution due to the amount of gasoline or other fuel you can safely store. Warning: Generators emit deadly carbon monoxide, so they should be run outside the house where there is sufficient ventilation.

Alternative Power Sources

Electricity can be generated using alternative sources like wind energy or solar energy. However, unless you go through great expense to outfit your home to function off the grid, these power sources have little practical use in an emergency blackout. The only exception would be a small solar panel, capable of charging rechargeable batteries used in radios, walkie-talkies, and flashlights.

Food

If the power outage continues for more than two hours, then the food you keep in your refrigerator could spoil. Perishable foods should not be held above 40 degrees Fahrenheit (4° Celsius) for more than 2 hours. To preserve as much food as you can during a prolonged blackout follow these steps.

Do not open the refrigerator or freezer. An unopened refrigerator will keep foods cold enough for a couple of hours at least. A freezer that is half-full will hold for up to 24 hours and a full freezer for 48 hours.

If it looks like the power outage will be for more than 2-4 hours, pack refrigerated milk, dairy products, meats, fish, poultry, eggs, gravy, stuffing and leftovers into one or more coolers. These can be used to refrigerate perishable food items after a power outage for several hours. If it looks like the power outage will be prolonged, prepare another cooler with ice for your freezer items.

If the outage continues for more than a day then eat the perishable food items first and save the canned goods you have stored for after these items have run out or spoiled.

Ideally, you should have a digital quick-response thermometer so that you can quickly check the internal temperatures of food for doneness and safety. If the internal temperature of perishable items has not risen above 40° F (4° C) for more than two hours it is probably still safe to eat.

If the food in the freezer has ice crystals and is not above 40 degrees you can refreeze it.

Riots

Riots can occur almost anywhere and for any number of reasons. You can be caught in a riot in three ways:

1. A riot takes place outside your home or workplace.
2. You are traveling and encounter a riot.
3. A peaceful assembly or entertainment event turns into a riot.

Generally, there are signs of public anger and violence a few days to a few weeks before the actual riot. Reading the newspapers and following the news may give you a warning about impending protests, rallies, and marches. Being informed and avoiding troubled areas is always your best defense.

What to do Indoors

If a riot occurs outside your home or workplace, stay inside. Typically, riots occur in the streets or elsewhere outside. Staying inside provides the best protection to wait out the riot. Keep doors and windows locked. Avoid watching the riot from windows or balconies, and move to inside rooms or at least away from windows and doors to minimize the risk of being hit by stones or bullets.

Search for, and mentally note, at least two possible exits in case you need to evacuate the building in a hurry. Be on the lookout for signs of fire. If the building is set on fire, get out quickly. If rioters are targeting the building and gain entry, try to sneak out or hide.

Check media sources for further information on the progress of the riot. Some riots have been known to go on for days. Contact police to let them know where you are and to request instructions on if and when to evacuate.

In public places, like restaurants and barbershops, pay attention to the flow of foot and vehicular traffic outside. Is there a sudden change in the pace or the rhythm? My wife and my youngest daughter went out to eat. Every so often, as I always do, I look out the window and study the movement of the streets. I listen to its sounds and feel its rhythm. After a while, I noticed a shift – more people were walking the street than normal. Then I noticed many more college-aged young men and women were out.

I told my wife it was time to go and then I told our server to bring the check and some "to-go" boxes.

I paid four our meals and we packed up our food. By the time we were ready to go, thousands of youth had taken to the streets, blocking traffic and scores of police cars and police motorcycles were approaching the scene.

We snuck out of the restaurant's side door, hopped in our vehicle and took side streets out of the area.

We had just escaped a heated gathering of young people protesting police brutality perpetrated against Black people and the lynching of a young brother in the Midtown area of Atlanta.

What to do Outdoors

- *On Foot:* Get inside and *stay* inside if you can. Find a retail store, office building, or coffee shop to get into and off the streets. Look for a rear exit to these buildings that will lead out to a back street where there are no rioters and carefully make your way home.

Try to look as inconspicuous as possible; slowly and carefully move to the outside of the mob. Stay close to walls or other protective barriers if possible.

Move away from the riot. The more time you spend in the midst of a riot, the greater your chances of being injured or killed. However, in most circumstances it is better to move out of a riot slowly. If you run, you will draw attention to yourself, so it is usually best to walk.

It can be dangerous to move against a crowd, so go with the flow until you are able to escape into a doorway or up a side street or alley. It may also be advantageous to stay with the crowd until you are certain you can safely escape because it will help you remain inconspicuous and improve your odds of survival if shots are fired. In addition, police may barricade side routes and ambush anyone seeking to escape the main mob. You do not want to be the only person trying to get past a police barricade.

Crowd movement is like currents in the ocean. In a large riot, the crowd of people in the middle will move faster than on the perimeter. As such, if you find yourself in the middle, you should not try to move in a different direction, but follow the flow and slowly make your way to the outside.

Avoid public transportation. Buses, subways, and trains will likely be out of service, and stations and depots will probably be packed with people. Even if you succeed in getting on a train or bus, rioters may stop it. Subway stations are particularly bad places to be, both because they are difficult to escape and because riot control agents – pepper spray, CS and mustard gas, and the like – are heavier than air and may drift down into subway stations and accumulate there.

Avoid any contact with riot control chemicals. Police may deploy "tear gas" – which is actually low-grade nerve gas. These chemicals can cause severe pain, respiratory distress, and blindness. Try to stay away from the front lines of a riot, and learn to recognize the signs that a riot control agent has been used. These signs include popping sounds made buy tear gas launchers, hissing sounds from tear gas grenades, clouds of white smoke, and sudden surges in the crowd.

- *In a Vehicle:* Avoid major roads, city squares, and other high traffic areas that are likely to be crowded with rioters. If possible, stick to less-traveled side streets to avoid the mobs.

  Do not stop your car. If you can drive away from the riot, drive quickly and try not to stop for anything until you have reached some place you know is safe. If people are blocking your escape route, honk your horn, and carefully drive through or around them at a moderate speed; they should get out of the way.

  Never drive towards police lines as this will be interpreted by the police as an intention to use the car as a weapon against them. They will open fire on you if they think you are going to run them down with a car.

  Also, avoid driving towards crowds if possible since this could elicit a violent response. There have been numerous cases of irate non-participants running down protesters. Any pushing though the crowd should be done with patience. Aggressive driving may anger the crowd into attacking you, your vehicle and your passengers.

  If you are in a car and the mob surrounds it, get out immediately. Staying in the car could be a fatal mistake, since rioters could roll the car over and set it on fire in seconds.

What to do at a Public Event

Be prepared. If you know an area is ripe for a riot but you cannot avoid traveling there, take some simple precautions to help protect yourself. Wear clothes that minimize the amount of exposed skin – long pants and long-sleeve shirts. Choose clothing that will help you blend in. Avoid looking conspicuously wealthy, as you are likely to draw the unwanted attention of opportunistic thieves.

When you attend a public event, make it a habit to check for exits and possible escape routes and safe havens. This is a good habit since, should there be a fire or terrorist attack, you will need to know this in order to evade trouble and evacuate the area.

Carry some cash with you in case you need to quickly arrange transportation, pay off looters, or bribe police at a checkpoint. If you are traveling abroad, register with your country's consulate and carry your passport and/or visa with you at all times.

If a riot breaks out in a stadium, quickly move to an exit. Do not run, however, unless you are in imminent danger; people are frequently trampled by stampeding crowds near exits.

How to Deal With Riot Control Agents

The term "riot control agents" (RCAs) refers to several gases commonly known as tear gas – these include pepper sprays, CS gas and mustard gas. Exposure to these chemicals can cause skin, nose, and eye irritation, nausea, and respiratory difficulties within minutes. In rare cases, RCAs can cause long-term health complications, blindness, and even death. The effects generally last less than half an hour but can be extremely uncomfortable.

The first defense is to try to stay out of the line of fire and away from the front lines of the rioters. If the chemicals are released in front of you, you should turn on your heels and run to get out of range. Try to get upwind of the point of release where there is fresh air.

If RCAs are deployed inside a building, get out as quickly as possible. The chemicals do not dissipate as they would outdoors, and the high concentrations can be extremely dangerous with prolonged exposure.

Get to high ground. RCAs are heavier than air, and the highest concentrations thus tend to be near the ground. Try to get to the highest point possible. This could be up a hill, atop a wall, etc.

If you are caught in a smoke cloud, soak a bandanna or other cloth in apple-cider vinegar or lemon juice and tightly cover your mouth and nose with it. Of course you would have had to bring these items in the expectation of rioting.

Finally, avoid wearing oil-based creams or sunscreens, as these aid absorption of the RCAs.

Chemical Attack

Chemical warfare agents are gases, aerosols, liquids or solids that have toxic effects on people, animals or plants. They can be dispersed by bombs, sprayed from aircrafts, boats, or motor vehicles, or poured into stream, rivers, lakes and other water supplies to create a hazard to people and the environment.

Some chemical agents are odorless and tasteless.

Exposure can occur through ingestion, breathing, absorption through the skin, and contact with the eyes.

Effects of these agents can include: breathing difficulties, eye irritation, skin abnormalities, nausea, respiratory problems, and chest or abdominal pains. These symptoms can occur immediately, within a few seconds, a few minutes, or delayed up to several hours or days.

Precise symptoms would depend upon the agent used, and the severity of the symptoms can depend upon the person's proximity to the contamination.

While potentially lethal, chemical agents are difficult to deliver in lethal concentrations and dissipate rapidly when dispersed outdoors.

Prevention and Defense

Check with your city or town to see if they have an evacuation procedure in the event of natural disaster or terrorist attack. If they do, then avoid using their recommended exits. The evacuation routes they suggest will likely become total mayhem as people panic, particularly in a major city. Depending on the nature of the chemical disaster, you may have to make the choice to evacuate or to stay put.

Another thing to check on is whether your city or town has any communal buildings that they plan to use as a shelter in the event of an attack. AVOID THESE! *Refugee* is synonymous with *slave*. Take New Orleans as an example:

People left homeless by Hurricane Katrina told horrific stories of rape, murder and trigger-happy police and military in two New Orleans centers that were set up as shelters but became places of violence and terror.

The refugees, who were waiting to be taken to sports stadiums and other huge shelters across Texas and northern Louisiana, described how the *Convention Center* and the *Superdome* became lawless hellholes beset by rape and murder.

Several residents of the impromptu shantytowns recounted two horrific incidents where those charged with keeping people safe had killed them instead.

In one, a teenager was run down and then shot by a New Orleans police officer; in another, a man seeking help was gunned down by a National Guard soldier.

In the case of the man who was murdered by U.S. soldiers, a young woman was being raped and stabbed in the *Convention Center*. The sounds of her screaming got to this brother, so he ran out into the street to get help from troops. He tried to flag down a passing military truck. They refused to acknowledge him, so the man jumped up on the truck. They acknowledged him then...and shot him dead.

The teenager was 16. He was just crossing the street. New Orleans police ran him over and then they got out of the car and shot him in the head.

The young man's body lay in the street by the Convention Center's entrance, covered in a black blanket, a stream of congealed blood staining the street around him. Nearby, his family sat in shock.

People in the Convention Center reported well over 20 bodies of adults and children stored inside the building in a makeshift morgue, but troops guarding the building threatened to beat any reporters who sought access to the "morgue."

People who tried to leave the Convention Center or Superdome were forced back inside at gunpoint – something troops said was "for their own safety."

At the Superdome, where as many as 38,000 refugees were held, the scene was one of abject filth. People sat amid heaps of garbage piled waist high. The stench of human waste pervaded the interior of the stadium.

At the Superdome's makeshift morgue, there were over 100 bodies. Two of the more well known residents were a young girl, who was found raped and murdered in the bathroom; and her rapist, who a crowd found and then beat to death.

As I said...do NOT become a refugee!

Signs of Chemical Attack

Since many chemical agents cannot be seen or smelled, you will have to rely on observation and information to recognize that you are in danger. The earliest signs of a chemical attack are birds dropping from the sky, or numerous dead squirrels and rodents scattered around. Birds and small animals are particularly susceptible to poison gas and would be the first casualties of a toxic contamination.

If you see a *single* person on the ground, choking or having a seizure, chances are that this individual is having a heart attack or epileptic seizure. However, if *several* people are down, coughing, vomiting, or convulsing, they are probably reacting to the presence of a toxic substance.

Evacuate the area immediately.

What to do During a Chemical Disaster

- *Outdoors:* If you are caught outdoors during a chemical attack or disaster the most important thing to do is to get a physical barrier between you and the toxic cloud. Get indoors quickly, preferably into a building but even being inside a car will help.

  If there is no safe building nearby, try to determine the direction of the wind and move crosswind. If you move down-wind you risk remaining exposed to the gas for a longer time. If you move up-wind you risk entering a more dense cloud of the gas. By moving crosswind you have the greatest chance of getting out of the cloud quickly because the gas will move with the wind along a relatively narrow line. Seek higher ground and avoid gullies, valleys and depressions since chemical gases tend to collect in these areas.

If you are in your car, stay inside and attempt to drive away from the cloud – again, crosswind, if possible. You should not try to shelter in a vehicle unless you have no other choice. Vehicles are not airtight enough to give you adequate protection from chemicals

Emergency First Aid Tip: In emergencies, dry powder such as flour, baking soda, detergents, or even soil can be used to significantly reduce the effects of chemical agents upon the skin. Pouring flour onto the chemical, followed by wiping the affected area with wet tissue paper is effective against the nerve agents *soman, VX,* and *mustard gas.*

- *Indoors:* If you come indoors after being potentially exposed to toxins, go immediately to *Decontamination.*

If you are indoors, stay calm but make sure to get your family and pets indoors as quickly as possible.

Since the best course of action is to stay where you are, take a few precautions to make your home as safe as possible.

Shut and lock all outside doors and windows. Locking them may pull the door or window tighter and make a better seal against outside contamination. Turn off the air conditioner or heater, ceiling fans and bathroom fans. If you have a wood stove or fireplace, close the damper and seal off any other place that air can come in from outside.

Choose a room in your house or apartment with as few windows and doors as possible and/or one that has access to water such as a master bedroom with a separate bathroom. Since most noxious chemicals and fumes are heavier than air the best choice for a safe room would be one above ground floor. (Note this is contrary to the advice given for other natural disasters such as hurricanes, or nuclear events, where the shelter should be low in the home.) In the room, you should also have a working landline telephone and/or a cell phone.

Bring your *Bug-In Bag* into the room if it is stored elsewhere. Also, include duct tape, scissors, towels and plastic sheeting. Cut the plastic sheeting to fit windows and doors and use the duct tape to seal the edges and hold the plastic in place. Also, tape over any vents into the room as well as electrical outlets or other openings. Wet towels can be stuffed under door cracks to help keep fumes out.

You can use the sink and toilet as you normally would, for hygienic purposes, but do NOT drink water out of the tap. Drink stored water.

Aftermath

Immediate symptoms of exposure to toxic agents may include blurred vision, eye irritation, difficulty breathing and nausea. A person affected by a chemical agent requires immediate attention by professional medical personnel. If medical help is not immediately available, decontaminate yourself and assist in decontaminating others. Decontamination is needed within minutes of exposure to minimize health consequences.

List Of Chemical Agents

- *Arsenic:* Dispersed in aerosol form. Symptoms: sore throat, vomiting, diarrhea, blood vessel damage, heart rhythm abnormalities, a decrease in white and red blood cells and skin abnormalities. Ingesting large quantities of this compound can result in death.

- *Chlorine:* Used as a gas. Symptoms: Chest pains, burning throat sensation and in some cases asphyxiation.

- *Cyanide:* Used in gas form. Symptoms: Lung problems, respiratory failure, heart problems and brain damage. Even a small amount of this agent, either breathed in or absorbed through the skin, can cause a number of health problems.

- *Lewisite:* Blistering agent. Symptoms: Blistering and lesions of the skin, blindness, lewisite shock, chronic respiratory problems and death. Contains arsenic and some of the effects are also similar.

- *Mustard Gas:* Blistering agent. Affects people through ingestion, skin contact, breathing and eye contact. Effects include skin abnormalities and blistering, respiratory tract problems, abdominal pain and nausea, swelling and irritation of the eyes, and fever.

- *Phosgene:* Choking gas absorbed through skin, breathing and eye contact, Symptoms: Chronic emphysema, chronic bronchitis, fluid on the lungs, breathing difficulty, heart failure, and skin lesions.

- *Strychnine:* Used in powder form. Symptoms: Breathing difficulty, respiratory failure, brain death, muscle spasms, and psychological problems.

- *Sarin:* Fast acting nerve gas. Symptoms: Paralysis, convulsions, extremely high, or low, blood pressure, abdominal pains, vomiting, chest tightness and unconsciousness.

Biological Attack

Biological agents are organisms or toxins that can kill or incapacitate people, livestock and crops. Biological agents can affect a population through natural person-to-person spread of infectious agents such as smallpox, and plague, or it can be released through industrial accident, bio-warfare or bio-terrorism. There are three basic groups of biological agents that could be used as weapons; *bacteria, viruses,* and *toxins.*

- *Bacteria:* Bacteria are small organisms that reproduce by simple division and are easy to grow. The diseases they produce often respond to treatment with antibiotics.

- *Viruses:* Viruses are organisms that require living cells in which to reproduce and are intimately dependent upon the body they infect. Viruses produce diseases that generally do not respond to antibiotics. However, antiviral drugs are sometimes effective.

- *Toxins:* Toxins are poisonous substances extracted from plants, animals, or microorganisms. Some toxins can be treated with specific antitoxins and selected drugs.

Biological agents can be used as a weapon using three methods of deployment.

- *Aerosols:* Biological agents are dispersed into the air, forming a fine mist that may drift for miles. Inhaling the agent may cause disease in people or animals.

- *Animals:* Some diseases are spread by insects and animals, such as fleas, mice, flies, and mosquitoes.

- *Food and water contamination:* Some pathogenic organisms and toxins may persist in food and water supplies. Most microbes can be killed, and toxins deactivated, by cooking food and boiling water.

Biological agents tend to break down quickly when exposed to sunlight and other environmental factors, while some, such as anthrax spores, are very long lived.

Preparation And Defense

- *Gas Masks*

In order for a mask to protect you against a bio-chemical attack you would need to carry the mask with you at all times – 24 hours a day, 7 days a week. Since biological agents are not immediately obvious and can have a delayed effect, you would therefore need to wear it at all times to be effective. In addition, a gas mask needs to be properly fitted to each individual, is expensive to purchase, and requires training to use. Thus, for all the time and effort invested for only a minor return in survivability, they are not cost effective.

An alternative to a gas mask is a *surgical mask* or one of the *respiratory protection masks* recommended for various construction and laboratory tasks. They can help to screen out particulate matter that might be in the air, but these do not provide ironclad respiratory protection. Make sure the mask fits snugly over the mouth and nose.

- *Antibiotics*

Most authorities recommend you do NOT keep a stockpile of antibiotics because adverse side effects may occur when untrained individuals self-medicate and because their overuse can reduce the ability of these drugs to work in serious health emergencies.

However, for many types of bacterial infections that can result from any injury, including bio-warfare agents, antibiotics can be the only treatment that could save lives. If you have someone suffering a life threatening infection, and the odds are against you being able to find professional medical attention for three or more days, then as a last resort, a course of antibiotics could save the patient. The danger in taking antibiotics is that a person may be allergic to that specific type. If you stockpile antibiotics, you need to do your research on the types and applications and ensure that whoever is taking them is not allergic to that type.

Signs Of Biological Disaster

It may not be apparent that a biological agent has been dispersed until people begin falling ill several days later. For most biological agents, the initial symptoms would resemble a flu-like illness. In such situations, the first evidence of an attack may be when you notice symptoms of the disease and you need to seek medical attention for treatment.

What To Do During A Biological Disaster

Biological disasters can take the form of infectious diseases or the form of toxic chemicals. If it is an infectious disease then you will likely not know whether or not your area has been hit or infected until after the fact. Once you have been informed or evidence leads you to suspect some agent is causing illness and death, then follow the same procedures as dealing with a *Pandemic.*

If the biological disaster takes the form of a release of toxic agents, follow the same guidelines for *Chemical Disasters.*

If the exact nature of the biological agents involved are unknown then employ the safety measures for both pandemic AND chemical disasters.

Emergency First Aid Tip

In emergencies, a disinfectant solution made from.05% chlorine bleach and water can be used to rinse your skin of infectious agents. However, do not the use solution on your face.

List Of Biological Agents

- *Toxins*

    1. *Anthrax,* in powdered form, can cause symptoms that include vomiting, fever, abdominal pain, skin lesions, diarrhea, and ultimately death.

    2. *Botulism* is highly toxic and can contaminate the air, resulting in inhalation botulism. Symptoms include blurred vision, swallowing difficulty, respiratory failure, paralysis, and muscle weakness.

3. *Ricin* can be used to contaminate water supplies, food or the air, through aerosol form. Symptoms include breathing difficulty, cough, nausea, sweating, low blood pressure, blue tinge to the skin, respiratory failure, circulatory failure, and death.

- *Viruses*

  1. *Plague*, symptoms include swollen glands, fever, exhaustion, headaches, breathing difficulty, coughing up blood and death.

  2. *Smallpox* is highly infectious. Symptoms include fever, headaches, rash and skin lesions, backache and fatigue.

  3. *Tularemia* is an organism that can be used in aerosol form to contaminate the environment. Symptoms include ulcers, swollen glands, fever, abdominal pains, vomiting and nausea, diarrhea, weight loss, headaches, fatigue, chills, pneumonia and possible death.

  4. *Viral Hemorrhagic Fever's* symptoms include fever, muscle weakness, fatigue, dizziness, bleeding under the skin, bleeding of internal organs,

bleeding from external orifices, shock, nervous system abnormalities, coma, seizures, and kidney failure.

5. *Cholera* is usually transmitted via drinking water. Symptoms can include diarrhea, vomiting, cramps, dehydration, shock and possible death.

6. *Brucellosis* can linger in the environment for a couple of years. Contamination through an aerosol form would be the most likely bio-terrorist route. Symptoms include fever, sweats, fatigue, weight loss, joint pains and headaches.

Nuclear_Attack

The possibility of having to deal with a nuclear disaster in one form or another is not beyond the realm of possibility. Such a disaster can come from a terrorist attack, an attack from a nuclear-armed nation, a nuclear power station meltdown or an accidental, or even intentional, detonation of a nuclear device by one's own government. Whatever the cause or origination of a nuclear event, the following procedures can increase your likelihood of survival.

Preparation And Defense

If a nuclear detonation takes place, it will be too late to start thinking about preparation – you should prepare now, however unlikely you think the prospect of a nuclear attack is.

Surviving a nuclear disaster requires advanced planning. There are three stages to a nuclear disaster that require three different strategies:

1. *Blast Stage:* Stay put behind solid protection.

2. *Fire Stage:* You will most likely have to flee.

3. *Fallout Stage:* The wind carries the radioactive materials from the nuclear detonation through the air to other areas. At this stage you may have to evacuate or stay, depending on the circumstances.

The first step is to assemble a *Bug-In Bag* should you need to shelter in place and a *Bug-Out Bag* in case you need to evacuate. Create a plan of action on what you and your family should do in the event of a nuclear disaster.

What To Do During A Nuclear Attack

A nuclear explosion creates a powerful blast wave that can destroy everything around through its enormous force. The initial flash of the blast can be so intense that simply to look right at it can result in blindness and permanent eye damage. It can also result in fire through the ignition of combustible material and this is a particular risk in the area close to the blast.

When the blast occurs, the first step for you and your family is to take shelter during and after the blast. Unfortunately, you will have mere seconds to decide. To survive the impact of the blast wave you are safer below ground level. If there is some advance notice or warning of an impending nuclear event then bring your Bug-In Bag and supplies down into your basement, crawl space, underground parking garage, or the lowest floor in your home. Stay away from windows and move to the interior of the building to put as many walls between you and the outside as possible.

If you are outside when a nuclear attack occurs, you should literally dive for cover and do not look up at the blast as this could blind you. Find a ditch, run to the nearest building or anywhere that you might be able to find shelter as low down as possible. If you are in a car, you should wind down the windows to avoid possible injury from breaking glass and get down on to the floor of the vehicle, shielding your face and eyes.

The second danger from a nuclear explosion is the risk of a firestorm, triggered by the blast and heat of the detonation. Fire is a high risk, particularly in areas close to ground zero. If you survive the initial blast but find yourself inside the fire radius, you will need to evacuate quickly. Keeping a Bug-Out Bag ready will be a lifesaver if you have to travel away from the city and survive in the wilderness for several days.

Once the initial explosion is over you will need to be prepared for nuclear fallout. There are two strategies to survive the final fallout stage:

- *Shelter in Place*

  This requires that you construct some form of fallout shelter. Fallout shelters can be constructed in the basement or backyard.

  You may have to be sealed in for several days, so you must ensure you have adequate supplies of food, water, cooking utensils, medical supplies, and some form of human waste disposal.

  The fallout from the first 24 hours following detonation is the most dangerous as these particles are still highly radioactive. Fallout can continue for months or even years. However, the fallout radiation levels decrease very quickly, and within a couple of weeks it is just a tiny fraction of the levels at the time of detonation.

  In an urban environment, you are most likely to have to shelter in place for at least a few days. While evacuating to a safer area that will not be affected by the fallout is preferable to being sealed in a small room for weeks, you may not have that option.

  In populous areas, the evacuation routes can be damaged or destroyed by the initial blast and the sheer number of people living and working in the city could mean that the streets become too jammed to evacuate. It is better to stay put than to run out of gas in an endless traffic jam and become stranded on a highway where you will be exposed and with few resources.

- *Evacuate*

  Ideally, it is better to evacuate the contaminated area and find shelter that is as far as possible from the blast and is upwind from the blast.

  Wind direction and weather patterns will determine the best direction to head toward. Listen to weather and news reports on your portable radio to plan where you should go.

  Fallout patterns typically resemble a feather shape with the point at ground zero and the plume going in the direction of the prevailing wind. Most wind patterns in North America follow a west to east direction. If a nuclear explosion occurred west of your current location, and the wind is blowing from west to east, then the best directions to take would be to the north or south, to take you out of the plume of fallout.

  You may need to stay away for a long period of time, depending on the extent and severity of the contamination. It is important to plan to evacuate to a retreat location that would provide both protection against contamination as well as uncontaminated food and water such as bottled water and tins of food that will last for a while. One possibility is to arrange to stay with friends or family in unaffected areas for the duration of the emergency.

If you or your family owns a cabin or cottage away from the affected areas, that would be an ideal retreat location. If you do not *own* any vacation property, you may be able to *rent* a cabin – or "occupy" one for the couple of months it would take for order to be restored.

Aftermath

After either sheltering in place or evacuating to a shelter your next priority will be to treat injuries and address health concerns. A nuclear disaster will create every type of injury, from fractures, lacerations, and burns to blindness and radiation sickness. To make matters worse, if a nuclear detonation takes place in an urban environment the destruction to infrastructure and emergency services combined with the high numbers of casualties will mean that medical help may take a long time in coming.

If you followed the advice in *Preparing for Disaster*, you should have a list of neighbors and their survival talents. Contact anyone nearby that has medical experience for assistance. If there is no medical aid available, then hopefully you have a comprehensive first aid manual and you must do your best to treat medical emergencies on your own.

As soon as possible, have everyone examined by a doctor, even if no one was injured by the blast. Possible long-term health effects from radiation exposure are another concern and should be addressed by medical professionals.

Emergency First Aid Tips

Radiation sickness can be identified by symptoms such as vomiting, diarrhea, fatigue, fainting, dehydration, hair loss, loss of appetite and bleeding from the nose, mouth, rectum or gums. Skin reddening, rash, severe burns and peeling are also possible external effects.

The first step to any treatment is *decontamination*, which means removing as many of the radiation particles as possible. Here are a few useful items to keep on hand:

- *Baking Soda:* For the external cleansing of radioactive particles, soaking in baking soda may help. Baking soda is said to pull out the radiation and help cleanse the body. Bathe only after you have followed the *decontamination* procedure below.

- *Potassium Iodide:* Potassium iodide targets the thyroid and slows the absorption of radioactive iodine into the bloodstream.

The radioiodine is eventually released from the body through the urine. Potassium iodide should be taken as soon as possible. You should take one dose (100mg) every 24 hours for not more than 10 days.

- *Prussian Blue Dye:* Prussian blue dye clears the radioactive elements cesium and thallium from the body. These particles are then excreted from the body through feces. Prussian blue is available only by prescription. The CDC has included Prussian blue in the Strategic National Stockpile (SNS), a special collection of drugs and medical supplies that the CDC keeps to treat people in an emergency. Prussian blue is given in 500-milligram capsules that can be swallowed whole.

- *Antihistamines:* Antihistamines help alleviate such symptoms as nausea and vomiting and help reduce hypertension and relax patients.

Decontamination

If you or someone in your family or group have been exposed to riot control agents, chemical toxins, biological agents, or nuclear fallout the first course of action is to decontaminate that person. Decontamination is essential to reduce and prevent further injury to the contaminated person and to prevent that person from contaminating others. The following procedure should work with all forms of contamination:

Decontamination Area

If you are returning to your home or shelter after being exposed to toxic agents, it is best to decontaminate everyone before entering the living areas in order to prevent further spread of the contaminants.

If you are decontaminating outside, make sure you do so downwind of your home and any people in the area. The wind can spread these agents further and contaminate everything downwind of you.

If, for safety reasons, you are restricted to decontaminating indoors, then find a room lower in the home that is the least used and has the least number of windows. A room with a sink and running water is preferable such as a laundry room or guest bathroom. Seal any windows and air vents to prevent toxins from spreading through the ventilation system.

If you are assisting in helping to decontaminate someone else, then take the following safety precautions: Wear latex or rubber gloves, surgical mask, protective eyewear, plastic shower cap or bandana to cover your head and hair, and protective clothing such as a raincoat or plastic poncho. After assisting someone else you should then self-decontaminate as well.

Procedure

- Remove all clothing and other items in contact with your body. In most cases, taking off your clothes will remove 80-90% of the potential contamination.

- Contaminated clothing that is normally removed over the head, such as T-shirts and pullovers, should be cut off to avoid contact with the eyes, nose, and mouth.

- Remove eyeglasses or contact lenses. Put glasses in a pan of household bleach solution to decontaminate. Throw contacts away.

- Put contaminated clothing into a plastic bag and tie it off. Depending on the nature of the toxin, these clothes may be washed later.

- Rinse yourself with *cold* water, starting from the head and working down. It is important that you shower; do not take a bath. Do not use warm water, since this will open the pores and aid absorption of the toxins into the skin.

- When rinsing your hair, make sure you bend forward so that the water runs off your head rather than down your face, where it could further contaminate your eyes and nose.

- Decontaminate your hands using soap and water.

- Flush eyes with lots of water.

- Gently wash face and hair with soap and water; then thoroughly rinse with water.

- If pain in the throat makes breathing difficult, gargle with water. Spit the water out – do NOT swallow it. Do this only if you are able to do so without choking.

- Decontaminate other areas of your body likely to have been contaminated. Blot (do not scrub or scrape) with a cloth soaked in soapy water and rinse with clear water.

- Change into uncontaminated clothes. Clothing stored in drawers or closets are likely to be uncontaminated.

- Once decontaminated, you should seek immediate medical attention.

Neutralize and Disinfect

After following the above procedures you may still have to take further precautions to ensure you are fully decontaminated and prevent re-contamination.

- ***Neutralize:*** A solution of 5% baking soda and water will help to neutralize the chemicals on the skin, especially the irritant type chemicals normally used in riot control agents, such as mace and pepper spray. Concentrate the solution on red or blotchy areas.

- ***Disinfect:*** For biological agents, hypochlorite solutions are effective in the decontamination of skin or other materials. Disinfectants that contain chlorine bleach will destroy most biological agents. Ordinary laundry detergent with real chlorine bleach can also be used.

  Be sure to dilute the solution in water before you use it on your skin and then rinse the solution thoroughly off your skin after use.

  You should use a 5% solution to decontaminate equipment and objects and a 0.5% solution to decontaminate your skin.

For exposure to a biological agent, you will need to wash yourself well with a chlorine solution for about 15 minutes. In the case of blistering agents, about 5 minutes should be enough. Never decontaminate your face using hypochlorite solutions. Wash instead with soap and water.

CHAPTER THIRTEEN
MARTIAL LAW

Martial law, meaning *military rule*, is a set of rules that are implemented when a nation's military takes control of the administration of justice. Martial law is imposed in response to civil unrest or riots, or during wartime, when foreign armies force the nominal administration to go into hiding or exile.

In cases of civil unrest and riots, the implementation of martial law is an ill omen, foretelling of tyrannical forces at work within the government. In democratic countries, the government, in theory, exists to provide the greatest common good for the greatest number of people. When large portions of the population become so disenfranchised that they riot, it is a sign the government has failed. Under most democratic constitutions a government faced with widespread unrest should resign and call a new election. If, instead, a government resorts to using the military to control the populace, then it has become a dictatorship by any other name. Regardless of the reason for doing so, the declaration of martial law is a serious indicator of a dysfunctional, thus dangerous society.

What To Expect

The first change to expect is that most, if not all, of your civil or constitutional rights will be suspended. Your freedom of speech, assembly, and travel, and your right to bear firearms are the first to go.

Typically, marches, strikes, and public gatherings of more than three people will be forbidden. Curfews will be employed, and various checkpoints will be set up at which you would need to provide identification. All of your firearms will be confiscated during house-to-house searches conducted by the military and the police.

Next, restrictions on power consumption, food, medicine, exchange of currency, and livelihood will be enforced.

Within hours of a state of emergency being declared, grocery store shelves will be bare because of sudden stockpiling efforts or looting. Electricity and fuel may be rationed. Hoarding – the storing of extra food in your home – may be forbidden and house-to-house search teams may confiscate foods stores.

Finally, whole groups of people will be rounded up at gunpoint and relocated to holding centers, like the Superdome in New Orleans.

The greatest dangers you will face under martial law are of being killed or incarcerated for breaking one of the new rules.

Preparation

Having a *Bug-In Bag* assembled is a vital component to surviving martial law. Restrictions and access to food and medicine, as well as power and fuel shortages, are likely. Your *Bug-In Bag* will provide you with some buffering from the impact of these shortages. Usually, the conditions under which martial law is declared will grow over time, giving the astute observer some advance warning. If you have reasons to suspect martial law may become a reality, then add to your Bug-In Bag supplies – increase your food and water stocks from three *days* to three *months*. Do the same for your medical prescription, and pet food requirements.

Also, be sure not to advertise the fact that you are stockpiling or taking precautions. Afterward, many will be enticed to snitch on your activities that, by then, the government will have declared illegal.

Compliance

Most people, being law-abiding citizens, will face a moral dilemma under martial law. On the one hand, many will want to comply with the new rules, on the other, history has repeatedly shown that during such times of turmoil governments have readily sacrificed innocent civilians to advance their agendas. Furthermore, under martial law, it is a certainty that little the government says, through their official broadcasts, will be true. You must judge carefully whether following government regulations is in your – or your family's – best interest. For example, should you agree to evacuate to a government relocation center or should you go into hiding?

Stealth

Keep quiet. Do not talk about your political opinions, or actions you are taking to protect your family.

A common component to martial law is snitch networks that use fellow citizens to spy on each other and report violations of martial regulations. It is an ugly side of human nature that ordinary people will often betray and inform on their own neighbors and family during dire social conditions. Limit what you say when you are questioned by anyone in so-called authority. Follow the same rules for *Dealing with Police* discussed in an earlier chapter and never volunteer information.

Avoid, where possible, any dealings with the authorities. If you know where street patrols, roadblocks, and surveillance cameras are, avoid going there. Practice *Social Distancing* and avoid public gatherings or protests and limit your travel to only the most necessary trips. It is important during such times to attract as little attention to you as possible.

Aftermath

If martial law is declared as a result of a natural disaster, terrorist attack or rioting then it will not last longer than a couple of months and the best advice is to keep a low profile and wait until normalcy resumes.

CHAPTER FOURTEEN
CORRUPTION

Corruption is an inescapable consequence of civilization. Seldom in the course of history have there existed states that were not corrupt. Corruption also poses one of the greatest threats to a civilization, as many ancient scholars well knew. Much of our ancestors' advice railed against corruption and the need for society, especially the rulers, to adhere to a code of virtuous conduct. That the wise advice of our elders and ancestors was ignored should come as no surprise – a corrupt society is the result of a predominantly psychopathic elite.

Corruption causes an attitudinal change of a society, whereby the prime motivation is a mercenary self-preservation. No longer motivated by a concern for society, nature, truth, justice, patriotism, honor, or pride in one's skills, corruption reduces all such concerns to *"What's in it for me?"*

Corruption can be instigated by either a rapaciously greedy ruling class, or by dwindling resources.

Signs Of Corruption

- **_Bribes & Kickbacks:_** A bribe is any form of monetary exchange paid to a government official in order to influence that person's decisions.

  Police are bribed to avoid criminal charges, judges are bribed to drop criminal cases, jailers are bribed for better treatment, bureaucrats are bribed to process papers, and to hand out government contracts, presidents and prime ministers are bribed to provide monopolies and business concessions.

  This form of corruption is made to sound less sinister by referring to the bribes as licensing fees, processing fees, administration fees, finder's fees, commissions, and campaign contributions.

  The business world's equivalent to the bribe is the _Kickback_. Here, the same pattern is repeated: developers pay kickbacks to landowners, architects pay developers, general contractors pay architects, sub-trades pay general contractors, sellers pay to buyers and so on. Kickbacks are referred to as sales commissions, finder's fees, handling charges, administration expenses, and rebates.

- **_Patronage and Nepotism_**: Corruption also increases the formation of tribal associations. This is the "Old Boy Club," or some form of "Fraternal Order." This practice contributes to the weakening of the social machine since less skilled and often incompetent people, whose only qualification for the position is membership in the club, replace skilled and qualified people needed to run the machinery. In addition, when an administrator's primary allegiance is his tribe, his decision-making ability is impaired. What is good for the tribe may not be good for the overall health of the rest of society.

In business, nepotism leads to the first generation suffering and sacrificing to build the family fortune; the second generation living off the interest and the third generation spending the principle and impoverishing the family once again. Everyone knows of a family-owned business that went downhill after the boss' son took over the business. Seldom is the son as hard working and shrewd as the father. By the time the grandson takes over the reins, he usually has no interest at all in the family business and will spend the company into bankruptcy, or sell off his shares. Instead of the business being run by those best qualified, it is run by those who assume control, not through skill, but by accident of birth.

Thus, patronage and nepotism causes the machinery of society to fall increasingly into the hands of under-qualified and inept administrators who make bad decisions.

- **_Gangsterism_**: As corruption increases so does the competition for dwindling resources. As the competition increases, the clubs and associations become more violent and engage in more activities that are criminal. Those that do not are swallowed up by those that do. Thus the Tongs, originally Chinese community welfare organizations, evolved into international crime syndicates. Sicilian community defense leagues evolved into the Mafia, while the most successful, long-standing Caucasian gangs evolved into political parties.

Gangs have always existed within large populations, but their power waxes or wanes because of government policies. As a government becomes increasingly corrupt, there is a corresponding increase in the profit to be had by circumventing government regulations. Naturally, this is illegal, so it is the criminal gangs who are best able to exploit this opportunity.

While Triads have always existed in China, their enormous power and influence came only after opium became widespread and then banned. Then, huge profits from drug smuggling allowed them to buy power even at the highest echelons. In America, it was the profits from running liquor during prohibition that allowed local ethnic gangs to coalesce into criminal syndicates.

Government efforts to exert stricter controls on criminal gangs causes the supply to drop and profits to increase, thus fueling even more of the criminal activity they sought to stop. The end game consists of several criminal warlords vying for control of the government. Indeed, it could be argued that what passes for American history is but a record of rival gangs fighting for power.

- **Black Market**: One way to circumvent corrupt institutions is by creating a separate underground economy known a "Black Market." Here, goods and services that are taxed, monopolized, or sold at extorted prices by traditional industries are provided by gang elements to bypass the usual kickbacks to government and business.

The *black market* has its foundation in excessive taxation or government restrictions on certain goods. Corrupt regimes all make the same mistake, when searching for more money from the populace to compensate for the losses of inept administration and corrupt officials, they resort to raising taxes. Modern governments have sought to disguise these tax increases by calling it different names – licensing, processing, accessing, service fees – but ALL money paid to a government is, in effect, taxes, regardless of what you call it.

Increasing taxes only works until it reaches a certain bifurcation point – its own critical mass – after which every increase in tax rate results in less money going into government coffers. The higher the taxes, the more people will become a part of the underground economy in order to evade taxes.

When the tax levels increase to the point many people will not be able to survive on what is left, they are forced into a black market economy in order to feed their families. At this stage, corrupt governments will step-up their tax-collecting program using police and military forces. Anarchy and war will soon follow.

Once greed and corruption have pervaded all facets of a society then everyone, even decent people, must take part in the system to survive.

Surviving Corruption

For over four thousand years, scholars and philosophers have lamented and sought a cure for greed and corruption. Everything has been tried – religion, morality, strict laws and harsh punishments – but these methods succeeded only briefly, if at all. While a morally upright person can succeed in fighting corruption within his or her own small sphere of influence, on the larger scale, little can be done other than trying to survive.

CHAPTER FIFTEEN
WAR

Around the time that agrarian societies first developed, there was also introduced a new concept, ownership of territory. Those ancient skills that were so necessary to the hunt were now put to a different use, the defense or acquisition of territory.

Archaeology shows that shortly after the invention of the grinding stone came the invention of defensive walls, after the invention of the plough the sword was invented. War has been a part of civilization since its invention and has plagued every generation since. There is a good chance that you or your children will have to deal with a war scenario. Those who can see the signs and make the effort to prepare ahead of time will have a better chance surviving until peace comes again.

Signs of Impending War

Before war breaks out, there are several social changes that can act as indicators of approaching war. They are as follows:

- **Social Strife**: Increase in angry demonstrations, strikes, marches, rallies, and public speeches. Every leader knows that, regardless of the internal troubles, a powerful outside enemy will have the effect of uniting the people against a common threat. However, once the threat is removed, the internal squabbles will soon resume.

- **Unemployment**: Watch for a dramatic increase in the numbers of unemployed young men. The aggressive energies of young men need the outlets of hard work, sport, and physical intimacy. When these traditional channels of energy are denied, the inevitable outcome is increased crime and social unrest. The ruling party may be tempted to diffuse a potential rebellion by creating a conflict to draw off extra labor.

- **Dwindling Resources**: Scarcity of resources, especially food staples, metals, and petroleum products, leads to high prices that devalue paper currency and rapidly increase inflation. It is no accident that past world wars were preceded by economic recessions. In psychopathic societies, when resources started running thin, aggression was a means of driving away excess populations into other unexploited areas. Now, there is nowhere else to go, so we have to stand our ground and slug it out.

- **Increased Patriotism:** Patriotism is the classical lure used to appeal to the traditional warrior ethic. Look for increased patriotic speeches, flag waving, slogans, songs, marching bands, propaganda, portraits of "Great Leaders" and "Heroes of the 'Homeland."

- **Increased Militarism:** Initially, there are military recruitment campaigns, followed by conscription, followed by press gangs. Look for increasing government spending on the military, greater military influence on foreign and domestic policy.

- **Choosing an Enemy:** Before war can be declared, the government must designate an enemy. Traditional enemies are usually ethnic so-called minorities within society or neighboring countries. When war becomes eminent, one or more of these "enemies of the state" will begin to receive greater attention, followed by a dehumanizing process. Afrikans in America are America's current designated "enemy."

- **Dehumanizing Potential Enemies:** In order to be able to kill another human being wholesale, you must first dehumanize that person. That is, you must view the other person as a symbol of something evil and/or subhuman rather than a real, feeling, human like yourself.

In war, this is accomplished through propaganda. The enemy is never portrayed sitting down to dinner with a loving family, laughing and playing with children. Instead, they are portrayed as monsters through the use of slanderous propaganda and rumor campaigns.

The truth is that the soldiers of most nations are young, naive men that are easily manipulated to do that nation's bidding, no matter how wicked. Whenever a government depicts an entire nation or people as evil and warmongering, they are employing propaganda to convince the people to support an attack on that country and to make it easy for young soldiers to commit murder.

Surviving War

The first step to surviving war is to never join the U.S., British, or any other armed forces of a psychopathic society, and dissuade anyone you care about from doing so as well.

Wartime can bring some or all of the previously discussed manmade disasters. If the fighting takes place near your home, you may face a chemical, biological, or nuclear attack. If the fighting is abroad, you may nevertheless have to deal with martial law and a climate of corruption. Surviving war requires you to adapt the strategies for natural and manmade disasters for each possible disaster as they develop.

As the signs of war point to its imminent arrival be sure to refresh and redouble your survival skills and supplies. Add to your emergency supplies, take extra first aid and wilderness survival training, re-establish connections with friends, family, and neighbors to assist each other both for moral and for resource support. Join or establish barter networks and try to find other sources for goods and services for times when traditional channels for those goods and services become scarce.

Nations at war will use all available resources to keep their armies supplied. This means there is often not enough left for the civilian population. To prepare against such an eventuality, you should begin to store supplies as the signs of war become evident. Stockpile food, water, medicine, fuel, and seeds – should the war last longer than your stores, you may have to supplement your nutritional needs by growing your own vegetables.

Convert some of your wealth into gold or precious stones, or likely barter items such as cans of coffee, sugar, cartons of cigarettes or ammunition. Hide these items in several locations or caches.

The best way to survive a war is to remain unheard and unseen, and wait for it all to blow over.

Should you need to evacuate, you need to prepare travel documents, and transportation. This could include everything from an extra car or boat to an extra pair of walking shoes. You will need to have stockpiled fuel stores to run the transportation since you may not be able to buy these during wartime. Since the journey may take longer than expected, due to interruptions in communications, the mining and bombing of roads and other misfortunes, you need to carry food, water, extra clothing, temporary shelter materials, and medicine to last through the journey.

Prepare a second safe place to run to should the fighting move closer to where you are currently living. This could be a cabin or farmhouse in the country or another home on a different side of town – make an arrangement with friends or relatives living in another part of the city or country that, should fighting occur near your home, you and your family can go stay with your relatives until it is safe to return and vice versa.

Also, construct a hiding place at your home and/or your safe house to store your supplies in. Troops passing through your area will send out scavenger teams looking for food and other supplies for the military. In addition, able-bodied men and women should stay out of sight since they may be conscripted into the military.

As the war lengthens, greater and more frequent atrocities will be committed by military personnel against civilians. The bombing, shelling and gassing of civilians have been recorded in every major conflict since recorded history as well as large scale enslavement and imprisonment, torture and rape.

In such cases, you may have to escape, evade, and go underground, or fight for your life and the lives of your people.

CHAPTER SIXTEEN
ESCAPE & EVADE

As much as we may fear and admire other predators, it is modern man that is the unrivaled top of the food chain; the apex predator.

As children, we learn to play games such as *Peek-a-Boo*, *Hide and Seek*, *Ringolevio* and *Tag*. Despite their innocent appearance, these games are, in effect, exercises to train our hunting skills. As these games suggest, man's favorite prey is man.

At some point, many of us will find ourselves pursued by our fellow man, whether by enemy soldiers or by criminals in the urban jungle. As a rule, the longer you can avoid capture, the greater your chance of survival, however, the longer you stay on the run, the greater your chances of succumbing to the elements.

Most escapees are caught because they are unable to deal with the everyday problems of survival on the run, not because their pursuers caught up to them. When you are on the run, even minor difficulties can become a major problem; small cuts become infected, cause fevers and threaten gangrene. The best pair of shoes can cause sores so that travel becomes agony. Water, when available, may cause diarrhea and stomach cramps. In the summer, flying insects have been known to drive men insane. In the winter, the cold saps your strength and your will to survive. In addition, caloric requirements increase dramatically. Under normal conditions, 2,500 calories per day is adequate to provide enough nutrition to keep you healthy, but on the run, you may need three times that amount of calories to maintain the same degree of health. Once you are ill from malnourishment or injury, your chances of survival drop rapidly. To be sure, your pursuers are also suffering from the same conditions, but they have the option to return to home base, have supplies delivered, and time to replenish and heal. The primary difficulty when being hunted is to continually have to find shelter and provisions.

To evade effectively, you must know what methods would be used in trying to capture you. You must learn the *strategies of hunters*. There are three strategies common to hunting: *track and kill, ambush,* and *bait and trap.*

Track And Kill

Track and Kill consists of tracking, stalking, and when you have the game in sight, killing. This method requires a great expenditure of energy and is therefore usually restricted to large game where the caloric gains exceed the caloric expenditures. Tracking and killing is used by the strong against the weak; the many against the few.

Success is dependent upon the perseverance of the hunter. The only drawback is time – if the pursued is clever enough to elude capture for an extended time, then the amount of energy expended by the hunter increases. Eventually, the expenditure will exceed the reward and the hunt will be called off. However, if the hunters are determined, at any cost, to succeed, then capture is inevitable.

Tracking Methods

- *Sight:* Sight is our most highly developed sense used to follow the target directly or to see indications of his recent passing through an area, such as dust clouds, boat wakes, swinging doors, car headlights in the distance, or the smoke or glow from cooking fires.

- *Sound:* If the target is out of sight, or when it is impossible to see clearly, then the brain's focus switches over to auditory detection. People entering strange environments in the dark automatically reduce the amount of noise they make in order to hear more clearly. In the forest, you can hear game running through the brush, or splashing across streams; on the street, you can hear heavy breathing reflected off the walls of buildings, the sound of cans being kicked along the street, or the sudden barking of dogs.

- *Smell:* Tracking by smell is usually accomplished by trained dogs that, depending on the weather, can follow a scent trail up to three days old. However, smell can alert YOU of the presence of someone nearby. For example, Vietnamese guerrillas seldom ran into an American ambush because they were alerted by the distinct perspiration odor caused by the meat rich diets of the American soldiers.

- *Signs:* Signs are indications in the environment, clues to the direction the game is fleeing. Signs include tracks and footprints, matted vegetation and broken branches, blood drops if the prey is injured, warm ashes of a cooking fire, warm beds and warm car engines.

- *Spoor:* An animal's highly evolved olfactory sense allows it to garner a great deal of information by smelling another's droppings. Many animals instinctively bury their spoor to avoid giving their presence away. Humans leave behind another kind of spoor: *garbage.* Even an amateur going through a week's worth of your garbage would be able to tell what you ate, your gender, your overall health, and your age group. Everywhere we go, we leave behind a trail of garbage, wrappers, containers, papers, cigarette butts, discarded clothing, business cards, and unpaid bills.

Evading Trackers

There are three tactics to evade trackers: *hide your tracks*, *leave false trails*, and *wear the pursuers down*. A combination of all three methods works best.

Hide Your Tracks: To leave no trails requires an acute self-discipline to monitor your own movement to reduce the number of clues you leave behind. The following are some general precautions to use:

- Walking: Be aware of where you step; try not to leave footprints in soft earth, crush small twigs, matte down grass, or break small branches. Traveling along rocky or swampy ground and along waterways, such as streams and rivers, are best for hiding footprints.

- Resting: Improvise a simple perimeter warning system such as leaving three or four patches of dry twigs along the trail at twenty-foot intervals so that you can to hear the approach of anyone following along the trail. Never leave anything lying around; you may have to move away quickly and not have time to clean up.

Choose a campsite that is not an obvious choice for shelter; for example, an isolated cabin should be avoided, since it would seem an obvious choice to anyone hunting you. Similarly, a small clump of trees in a desert, a small clearing in the bush, a small island in the swamp, all would provide a comfortable shelter, and it is for that reason that these areas are searched first. The rule of thumb is: *the more unpleasant the location, the less likely it will be searched.*

When breaking camp, if no one is aware of your presence, maintain secrecy by cleaning and hiding your campsite. If you are being pursued, set up booby traps and plant false trails before leaving.

- Camouflage: Always try to camouflage yourself, your equipment, and your campsites – if the pursuers are able to catch up with you, you may still have the chance to hide. To camouflage yourself, take off your outer clothing and roll it in the mud, stomp it into the grass, soak it in the swamp and kick it around until your clothes are filthy. To blend in with your environment, you must *become* the environment. The same applies to your equipment. Check all metal, glass, plastic and other shiny surfaces such as belt buckles, glasses, pack frames, buttons and grommets. A reflective surface can catch the sunlight and signal your presence from miles away. These surfaces should be covered over with material or mud. Also, be sure to strap down, tape down, or dampen any equipment, such as cooking pots or tools that make a rattling noise.

Hunters always move up against, or diagonally across, the wind so their scent does not alert the intended game. However, if you are tracked by dogs, the opposite is true – move downwind, crossing water as often as possible. A simple rule to remember is to *hunt with the wind in your face, and run with the wind at your back.*

Leave False Trails: NEVER head directly for your shelter. Instead, make a couple of changes in direction before heading towards your final destination. False trails should be left anytime you change direction or come across intersecting paths. There are two ways to leave false trails: *backtracking* and *misdirection.*

- Backtrack: Used only if you have already gained a significant lead and can afford the time it takes to go over the same piece of ground twice. *Backtracking* means to return the same way you came, being careful to hide any sign of your return, and to then continue in a different direction. Those following you will eventually find your tracks end.

The standard procedure for trackers is to continue along in the same direction the tracks had been leading in order to pick up the trail further along. When they are unable to pick up the trail again, they will return, this time searching along edges of the path for signs that you may have cut off from the trail somewhere along the way. This costs the pursuers a lot of time and energy. Remember, the greater the cost it is to catch someone the greater the chances they give up the chase.

Backtracking is most effective when on soft, muddy, or sandy terrain. Since this type of terrain makes it easy to follow someone's tracks, it is likely that the pursuers are watching for footprints more than any other sign, so they are more likely to follow the false trail.

- Misdirection: Another method is to leave false clues. For example, if you come to a fork in the trail, drop a personal item such as a piece of garbage or shred of clothing along one path then backtrack and take the other path. Those following you will see the item and deduce you went up that path.

  However, if you know the trackers are experienced, back track once more and go along the original path where the item was planted. The purpose of this double play is because an experienced tracker would recognize the planted item so near the fork of a trail to be too coincidental, and would choose the other path.

Another tactic is to hang some strips of cloth or a couple of pieces of metal, (spoons, and tin cans) from a tree branch slightly off the trail in the thick foliage, so that when the wind blows through the branches it will make an unusual noise or movement. Those following will waste time carefully checking out the source of the unnatural sound or movement in the bush.

Wear Down The Trackers: The third strategy is to wear down the trackers *by leaving behind booby traps* or, if traveling in a group, *leaving men behind in ambush* to delay the enemy. Those following will become wary and suspicious of traps or ambushes and this will slow them down.

Leaving behind just one booby trap will have the desired effect since, while you are free to move as fast as *you* can, the *pursuers* must slow down and cautiously check ever step they take for fear of walking into another trap.

Booby traps need not be complex or even dangerous, anything unusual such as some pointed sticks stuck in the ground or a strange looking parcel left in the path will arouse suspicion. Planting even a slight doubt in the mind of your enemy is a great advantage.

- Ambush: The *ambush* requires less expenditure of energy than *tracking and killing,* so it is used more frequently. The principle advantage of an ambush is the element of surprise – allows the weaker to overcome the slightly stronger; the few to overcome the many.

In order to set-up an ambush, the hunter must know the habits of her prey, where and when it eats, drinks, and sleeps, and the trails that it travels upon. Knowing these habits, the hunter sets up an ambush in an area he knows the prey will eventually pass by.

The drawback to an ambush is the need for concealment. Once you are detected, the element of surprise is lost. As a rule, the longer someone must wait in ambush, the more likely that they will be detected. Those waiting will get restless, the limbs become stiff from inactivity, the weather conditions may cause discomfort, and eventually they will have to eat and relieve themselves. All this activity increases as time goes on, and will eventually warn off the target.

Since there is a limit to the amount of time a pursuer can wait in hiding, an ambush must be set up near an area frequented on a regular basis, such as watering holes, trails, and cleared ground.

Avoiding An Ambush

Ambushes are planned in coordination with your routines and habits. To avoid an ambush, avoid routine. Take different routes both to and from home base, alternate the times when you sleep and wake. Do not always go to the same source of supplies and never implement the same strategy twice in a row.

- Set up a Red Flag: A *Red Flag* is any innocuous item that appears commonplace, but is placed in a specific position so that if someone enters the area, they will disturb the item's position and alignment. This disturbance will go unnoticed by the intruder, yet will alert you that someone has been – or *is* – there. For example, place a small branch across the trail or entrance to your camp in such a way that anyone entering would move the placement of the branch, unconscious of its significance.

Other methods include placing a piece of scrap paper inside the doorjamb when you close the door. The paper will drop to the floor unnoticed by someone else opening the door but will immediately alert you that someone has been there. Another method is to sprinkle a light dusting of talcum powder along a tile floor, or on top of filing cabinets, which looks like dust, and will reveal finger and footprints of anyone disturbing the room.

Always approach a base with caution. Check for signs of entry and do some reconnaissance before entering. Pass by home base as though you are heading for a different destination so that you can observe the area and then backtrack to base. If your red flag has been tripped, back off and wait. The longer you wait and watch, the greater your chances of spotting an ambush.

When traveling in a group, employ a *diamond formation*. Send scouts ahead to search for traps and ambushes, have outriders on the flanks, if possible, to prevent being cut off, leave a rear guard to use harassing and delaying tactics against possible pursuers.

If you must enter an area where you suspect an ambush, then use the *Shadow Horse* technique. This tactic comes from a hunting technique utilized by the ode ("hunters") of the ancient empire of Oyo, West Afrika. When using *Shadow Horse* – called "Ojiji Esin," in Yoruba – the ode would dismount and then walk beside their horses keeping the horses between them and their prey, which allowed them to get within close enough with their bows to shoot without spooking the prey.

This tactic can be applied in other ways, using the basic principle of hiding behind something common and non-threatening. Send in a third party to trigger the ambush and draw the attention, and then take advantage of the ensuing confusion.

- Bait And Trap: Bait and trap requires only the energy needed to construct and set the trap.

Traps can be used by the weak to overcome the strong and by the few to defeat the many.

Traps can vary from simple to complex constructions capable of tremendous destruction. There are usually two components to a trap, a *lure* and a *trigger*. Bait used to lure animals is usually food, bait used to lure humans includes money, power, sex, recognition, drugs, and anything FREE.

Like an ambush, a trap needs to be set near an area frequented by the intended target, but unlike an ambush, a trap need not be limited to the amount of time it waits.

The disadvantage of a trap is that it usually cannot discriminate between friend or foe, so it poses a hazard to both the intended target and any innocent party inadvertently setting it off.

Avoiding Traps: Like ambushes, most traps are laid between home and sources of supply. The presence of any sort of bait should alert you to the possibility of a trap. *Bait is anything you would want.*

Military demolitions experts have been known to booby trap food rations, weapons, equipment, and even children's toys. Finding supplies when on the run should always trigger caution. Beware of chance coincidences, unexpected windfalls, and new friends. One must train to develop a natural tendency to resist immediately reaching out for something one wants. The more you want it, the more cautious you should be.

If you suspect a trap, use the scapegoat strategy. The scapegoat suffers the consequences intended for others. In this case, the scapegoat is anything or anyone that will spring the trap and suffer the effects intended for you. This could be a stick thrown at a trip wire, a stray dog chased through a minefield, or a pizza delivered to your house.

Urban E & E

The above advice applies to evading in a wilderness environment, as well as in an urban environment.

Few societies have not had incidents of forced labor, conscription, internments, as well as government confiscations of personal property, bank accounts, and illegal search and seizures. History shows that every society undergoes occasional civil disorder and tyranny. For this reason, knowing some of the basic strategies of evading in an urban environment could prove vital to surviving such turbulent times.

Hiding Your Urban Tracks

In the urban environment, tracks are left in the form of computer records. Every time you use your name, there will be a trace left of your activities. The use of credit cards, gas cards, bank accounts, drivers licenses, social security numbers, library cards, social media, clubs and professional associations, telephone numbers, health cards, passports and birth certificates will create a record each time you use them. This information is readily available to anyone with the determination to retrieve it.

Under normal conditions, these records are benign, but during times of civil disorder, such information can be used to track down and exploit targeted groups or individuals.

- **Monetary Exchange:** Lessen your use of checks, money orders, or credit cards. Pay for things with cash or barter whenever possible. Never sign your real name on receipts and destroy the receipts you receive. (If you are captured, those receipts could help reconstruct your past activities and ensnare others.)

- **Changing Identities:** Use different names for different situations. For example, when you travel, you may use the name Walker, in restaurants and bars the name Cook, when shopping the name Green. The use of such names, in addition to making it difficult to discover your habits, also helps to serve a reminder to keep track of the different aliases. If you are in a group of people and someone recognizes you as Mr. Cook, you would know that you met that person in a bar or restaurant and you would then know which cover story to use when speaking with him or her. Maintaining consistency in your cover story is important.

- **Camouflage:** As in the wilderness, in the urban environment you must blend in with the surroundings. If you are heading for the business district, a suit and tie is camouflage; if you are heading for the country, overalls and boots are camouflage. Continually change your outward appearance and mannerisms. People recognize and remember each other more by what they wear and what they do than what their physical features are. It is much easier to identify someone who is wearing a red jacket and blue jeans with a nervous twitch than by a physical description.

When in doubt, wear the uniform of a technician, doctor, rescue worker, ambulance driver, or road crew. A uniform indicates that the wearer is an authority in some field and people are conditioned to obey this authority symbol. However, stay away from police or military uniforms as most armies have a policy of shooting anyone caught in their own uniform. There are also civil penalties against wearing a disguise, but if the disguise allows you to avoid capture, the penalties are moot.

If you are in a foreign country, it is safest to stay in areas frequented by foreigners. A stranger in the countryside is easily noticed.

In a pinch, you can also feign insanity – pretend to speak to an imaginary friend and never acknowledge the presence of others. People will take you for a nut and no one will ask serious questions, as they will be anxious to ignore you.

Leaving False Urban Trails

- ***Dead Letter Box:*** In the business world, false trails are better known as offshore bank accounts, subsidiaries, shell companies, holding companies, and trusts. These are employed by the rich and corrupt to hide their wealth in order to evade paying taxes, creditors, court judgments, alimony, insurance, and other costs.

  For those of more modest means, false trails can take the form of post office boxes, answering services, and business centers. By doing business under assumed names that can only be traced to a post office box or answering service you can monitor anyone taking an interest in you without exposing yourself. If those pursuing you overcome the dead letter box obstacle, you can fall back on attorneys to stall pursuers while you seek other means of escape. This is the method most often employed by petty confidence men and small businesses evading creditors.

- ***Transportation:*** Change your modes of travel regularly. Change license plates on cars and/or trade cars in for other makes and colors. When talking to gas station attendants or ticket cashiers, casually reveal a false destination. Those following and questioning witnesses will be given wrong or contradictory information. When buying bus or railway tickets, book the ticket for one stop further along the route than your true destination. Anyone wishing to ambush you will rendezvous at the wrong location, or if following you, they will relax their vigilance until nearing the final destination, unaware that your true destination is sooner than expected. Take advantage of their inattention to escape.

- **Misdirection:** This involves creating a fog of misinformation around you. Not telling the truth about where you live, where you are going, or what you are doing. Allow people to make their own conclusions. Anyone hunting you will receive conflicting information about your activities. Without discernable habits and schedules, it is more difficult to track, ambush, or trap you.

- **Losing a Tail:** The first step in losing a tail, is knowing you have one. To find out if someone is following you, backtrack and see if anyone backtracks with you. Walk down the street and then pretend you forgot something, cross the street and return in the same direction you came from. Anyone following you would have to turn around and cross the street as well, not something you can do without being noticed. In addition, by walking back you will be able to identify the tail.

Another method is to use reflective surfaces to look around without *appearing* to look around. Stop in front of a store window as though you are looking at goods while using the window's reflective surface to scan the background behind you. Pretend to look at your watch and use the glass lens as a mirror, or pretend to clean your mirror lens sunglasses to see behind you.

The basic strategy to lose a tail is to make the terrain more difficult to traverse by leaving behind obstacles. If you are on foot and those following are in a car, use footpaths. Go through alleys, into buildings, stores, shopping malls and lose yourself in the crowd. If those following are also on foot, go somewhere that requires a paid admission, like a subway train or movie theatre. The admission process incurs a non-negotiable time delay, while the tails are waiting to pay for admission, move quickly out a side or back entrance while they are still engaged at the entrance. If the tail is of the opposite sex, go into a busy public washroom and look for a service exit, window, or fire escape.

Misdirection can also be used when passing through a room: open the door but leave through a window or another door, or vice versa.

Avoiding Surveillance

Many countries routinely put their citizenry under surveillance. This includes bugging hotel, conference, and meeting rooms, and telephones; and reading mail correspondence.

In addition, many different people may be employed as informants, such as hotel staff, taxi drivers, tour guides, moneychangers, and even beggars and prostitutes.

Totalitarian governments also employ the common people in *neighborhood watch*-type groups that are charged with reporting all sorts of suspicious behavior. These informants may be encouraged to snitch out of patriotic duty, rewarded with money, made to feel they are important, or do so to avoid persecution, or prosecution, themselves. In a psychopathic society, this creates an atmosphere of distrust.

To avoid eavesdropping devices, do not use any electronic communication to discuss any secrets, or anything of high importance. If such communication is unavoidable, use a prearranged code system that could pass off as innocuous chitchat. For example, to express danger or a warning, you could say "It hot as hell outside," or "We lost that sale." It is not difficult to improvise any number of messages around such talk provided both parties have had time to set up the basic groundwork for the code. The same code can be used in written communications as well. If the communication is ongoing however, make sure to change the codes as often as possible since *every code can be broken.*

Avoiding an Urban Ambush

In the city, ambushes are set up near homes and offices, bars, clubs and vehicles. The salesperson ambushes his customer at home; court clerks serve subpoenas at the office; the police arrest people at their favorite hangout; muggers wait near parked cars.

The rules for avoiding an ambush are the same in the wilderness AND in the streets. Take different routes to and from home base; never head directly to a destination; and use extra caution every time you are near your home, workplace, shopping, and getting in and out of a vehicle. Stop and survey the area before entering and leaving these locations; leave and check *Red Flags*. If anything seems out of place, wait it out or leave.

Avoiding Urban Traps

The presence of any sort of bait should alert you to the possibility of a trap. Traditionally the bait used to lure prey in the urban environment is money, sex, or something FREE.

- **Money:** Common ploys include a dropped wallet, a sudden windfall, or a chance to earn money illegally. In con parlance, these traps lure suckers into the con game and are known by such names as 'The pigeon drop', 'The magic wallet', and 'The inheritance game'. Common sense states that everything has its price, making 'easy' money or getting more than fifteen percent return on your investment should trigger a warning.

- **Sex:** The second most popular bait. In the field of espionage, it is known as the 'Honey Trap' and is used to extort and blackmail the victim into handing over information. In confidence games it is known as the 'Badger Game' and is used to extort and blackmail the victim into handing over large amounts of money. If you find attractive men or women suddenly wanting to take you to their room and you are not terribly good looking, be suspicious. The variations on the honey trap are endless.

- **Something For Nothing**: Used in the same way as money but using merchandise or services as the bait. The key word is free. It seems to be an irresistible lure offering something for free.

- **Drugs:** The most effective of traps since once addicted, the victim no longer needs to be lured through artifice but is drawn into the trap over and over again through the urging of his own nervous system, overriding the conscious control mechanisms. The basic trap works as follows, victim is befriended by a gregarious outgoing sort of person who casually introduces the drug to the victim under the banner of joie de vie, initially free until the addictive effects begin to take hold. Then the friend turns into a tyrant using access to the drug as his base of power.

What To Do If You Are Captured

Whether you are captured by police or military forces, kidnappers, or terrorists, the methods of incarceration follow a common pattern. The following are general tactics that can help keep you safe when you are captured.

- *Negotiate*
  If capture seems inevitable, negotiate terms of "surrender." Negotiating offers the pursuers an end to the trouble in exchange for "better treatment" on your behalf. Of course, to expect your enemy to give you better treatment after you have submitted to your own enslavement is foolish, at best. Negotiation should only be used to stall your enemy if you expect reinforcements, or, to create an opportunity to deliver a final blow to the enemy, or to free your comrades.

- *Cooperate and Play Dead*

If you have been caught by surprise and negotiating surrender is no longer an option, then the first tactic is to pretend to cooperate, and to appear exhausted and injured. In this way, you appear less of a threat, which will allow the pursuers to relax their guard.

If you fully expect to be beaten, tortured and probably killed, strike hard, fast and without mercy when they leave an opening in their defenses.

- **Stall and Delay**

   Ask for medical treatment. If you can be transported to a medical facility, you increase the possibility of finding an opportunity to escape since security is never as tight in medical facilities as it is in other institutions. You want to avoid being processed as long as possible – the longer you are in custody, and the further along you are processed, the tighter the security. If you are not already injured, fake an injury.

- **Let Your People Know Where You Are**

   As soon as possible, make contact with the outside world through family, friends, comrades, and attorneys. Have them contact the authorities to inquire into your situation, post bail, hire lawyers, or bribe jailers. The more people that know where you are, and express their concern for your health to the people holding you, the less chance of you *disappearing.*

- **Make Friends**

  Most escape plans require inside help – the assistance of other prisoners and maybe even some guards. That means making friends with those who are able to assist you. Play on national, religious, and philosophical sympathies, and mimic the behavior of those you want to befriend. Of course, the best way to make "friends" when you are a captive is to have *money.*

The Gray Man

The *Gray Man* – or Gray *Woman* – blends into the background by not drawing attention through unusual behavior, manner, or dress. The Gray Man is really something you are; not something you DO and NO ONE can be Gray in every situation. A Black man in a rich, Caucasian neighborhood WILL get noticed, no matter how nice his sharkskin suit, or how fly his Rolls Royce.

Blending into a crowd is called becoming "gray."

There are people moving around us every day whose physical presence is so plain, so non-stimulating, that we ignore them. They are, for all intents and purposes, invisible to us. We want to emulate these people in a crisis.

The problem is, people have never *seen* a Gray Man or Woman to emulate, unless you have been *trained* to see them. Because, if you casually notice them, they aren't gray at all.

The brain remembers whatever significantly stimulates it. If there is no stimulus, there is no remembering. The brain contains a filter for all sensory input called the *Reticular Activating System*, or *RAS*. Your eyes send a complete stream of data down the optic nerve. The RAS scans that data and determines what parts of it to filter and what parts to pay attention to. This allows the brain to conserve energy by not having to process all the visual data it receives.

First, the brain looks for threats. The RAS will send data related to fast movement, threatening movement and movement on paths that will intercept your own. It also looks for bright colors, human shapes, reflections, bright light, implied movement and other things that stimulate the brain. The RAS ignores areas of continuous color, shadow, dull, natural colors, slow movement and movement off your path.

The RAS is a very effective filter for sound input as well. It filters sounds that are unnecessary for us to notice, such as the sound of the refrigerator running, but alerts us to sounds that may represent a threat, such as the sound of someone trying to jimmy a window at night.

I have a close friend that lives on the Westside of Chicago – my hometown, but I have lived in Atlanta since 1999. I was on the phone with him one day. A police car went by on his end. The sound of the siren, via the phone, was incredibly loud in my ears. I interrupted him and told him to wait until the pigs went by.

"What pigs?" he said. "This ain't Atlanta; pigs don't just run up and down our blocks. You can find plenty pig at these rib shacks on every corner, though."

The sound of the police car was so common on the Westside of Chi-Town, he filtered it out completely...and pigs do NOT "run up and down our blocks" here in the ATL, either.

So what does the RAS have to do with going gray? It's simple: to make yourself invisible to predators, don't trip their triggers. If you do not create a stimulus that the predator can key in on, you are invisible to him.

Just like my friend, who could not hear the police sirens, a Gray Man or Gray Woman moves around our awareness without triggering any alarms.

The Art of Blending

How is this accomplished? Just blend in. It seems simple, but there is actually an art to this.

- **Features:** The best Gray is ordinary in every respect. He is of average height and weight; he has no obvious physical features that draw attention. This can be cultural. For example, in some areas or cultures, wearing a full beard might be the style, like among Muslims or Hebrew Israelites, and a clean-shaven face would stand out, while in other areas, or cultures, a clean-shaven face would be the norm, such as in the Nation of Islam.

- **Dress:** Refrain from wearing any sort of logos, be it USPI, FTP, NOI, the company you work for, athletic teams, or anything like that. Go "sanitized" – strip any identifying materials from your clothing or gear. For example, if, during a disaster, you're wearing an *Atlanta Hawks* hat; someone may also be a fan – I don't know *why* they would be, but it happens – and notice you. Your hat created stimulus. Now, they come over and strike up a conversation. You are in a bad way and about to have a bad day once he notices your backpack and all your other gear.

For the most part, natural and neutral colors work best – browns, grays and dark blues. T-shirts with sayings or photos or strong stimuli WILL be noticed and remembered. Jeans and Khakis are acceptable as long as they aren't too tight, or falling off your ass.

The standard "uniform" for military-minded civilians consists of 5.11 Tactical pants, referred to by some of my friends as "shoot me first pants," a khaki cotton button-down shirt with epaulettes, Oakley shades, desert combat boots, and a shaved head. Add to that a nice MOLLE backpack, and you have "target" written all over you.

The Unprepared will believe that you have some very cool gear in that pack; they will want what's in it and they will go after it...and *you*.

Stay away from ALL tactical gear, especially tactical footwear. Dress for the occasion. If you're going to a formal dinner, dress formal. Dress for the season you are in. Do not wear a jacket in the summertime. Stay away from fashionable hair styles. A mohawk will not work, even if you're wearing the best Gray outfit. Avoid revealing clothing that may draw the attention of others. Also, remember to look non-threatening.

- **Mannerisms**

Since the Gray attract no attention, their mannerisms must be small and discreet; no sweeping gestures. Energetically, the Gray is withdrawn. He or she does not project confidence; he or she does not project weakness, either. He or she does not look around much and avoids eye contact, unless the people he is around look around a lot and stare people in the eyes.

- ## *Movement*

One of the key elements of camouflage is learning to match your movement to the *baseline.* If you spend any time in a city, you will notice that every neighborhood has a unique flavor – THAT is the baseline. It refers to the sound, motion and activity level of the neighborhood in a normal situation. The speed at which people move, the way they gesture, the volume and speed with which they speak. All these elements and many more make up the baseline. You can learn the baseline for a given neighborhood by sitting somewhere and watching.

Matching the baseline is probably the single most important task of personal camouflage and going Gray. Learning to walk like the natives walk will hide you better than just about anything else.

- ## *Route*

A key element in avoiding trouble is to not go where trouble tends to be. This means you must know the terrain like a native. You must know what neighborhoods are relatively safe and which ones to avoid. You must know roads and routes, locations of police stations, gas stations, convenience stores and emergency clinics. You should know what areas have street lights at night and which are dark. Know where the choke points are and where the police are likely to set up blockades. Being Gray means avoiding trouble by not going where trouble is, unless absolutely necessary.

Learning to See the Gray Man and Woman

To learn to see the invisible Gray, go to a public area with lots of foot traffic. Sit back and watch the crowd. As a person walks by, notice the stimulus that drew your eye. In your mind (not out loud), create an insult about that person's stimulus. The more outlandish the better – the purpose is to pound into your consciousness the stimulus: what you notice about each person. Then, after a few minutes, someone will walk by and you will not find anything – nothing to make fun of; nothing to ridicule. Pay attention to THAT person. Observe them carefully. See how they move, what kind of energy they project. See how they interact with others, what they pay attention to (or not). If possible, follow them for a bit. Observe their movements. The key to becoming a Gray lies in your ability to observe and mimic.

The Gray is the person who moves around the periphery of our awareness without creating any stimulus. This makes that person invisible for all practical purposes. Being invisible will greatly reduce the risk of falling prey to predators when this thin veneer of society peels away and reveals the ugliness and evil that lies underneath.

Escape Tactics

Although the specific details of an escape plan would be dependent on the circumstances, they all employ one or more of the following strategies:

- *Diversion:* A diversion, timed to occur at the most critical point in the escape, is used to draw attention away from you. Common diversions include staged fights or riots, false medical emergencies and accidents, alluring women, and the all time favorite, fire. The power of fire is that it cannot be ignored or dealt with later; it is, therefore, a sure-fire way to attract attention, cause panic, and draw off manpower.

- *Injuring Yourself:* This is a classic technique whereby you fake an injury, or even death, to escape. Methods include feigning insanity, or an epileptic seizure, consuming noxious substances to make you ill, and literally shooting yourself in the foot.

  WWII POW's smoked sugar in their tobacco, which gave them symptoms similar to tuberculosis. Prisoners in the notorious French penal colony at Devil's Island were known to cut their Achilles' tendons in order to avoid the grueling jungle labor that was the major cause of death.

The objectives of this strategy are to get you moved to a medical facility where conditions and/or opportunities to escape improve, to be relieved of having to do hard manual labor, or to be released, because your captors think you're dead or as good as dead.

- **False Flag (Disguise):** Prison uniforms are designed to be noticeably different from the type of clothes normally worn by civilians, making it easier to recognize and differentiate prisoners from guards, visitors, and maintenance staff, and to identify escaped prisoners.

  However, this can work against the system. People usually notice external clothing more than they notice physical characteristics. As long as you do not wear prison clothes, you will not look like a prisoner. The most common escape tactic has been to steal or manufacture a copy of the guard's uniform and walk out at the end of the shift. Other disguises include maintenance, delivery, medical, and religious personnel, or the opposite sex.

  Uniforms can be smuggled in under the clothes of visiting relatives or friends or, if security is too strict, a last resort is to change clothes with the visitor. If outside help is unavailable then uniforms may be bought or stolen from guards. A last resort is to alter the prison clothes. For this, you will need needle and thread, clothes dye, and badges, buttons, and nameplates - the little extras that can add authenticity to the disguise.

- **The "False Double" Strategy:** This is the classic of escape strategies and is familiar to anyone who has been late for work and has to punch a time clock – you have someone else clock in for you.

  In prison, this means having someone else stand roll call for you. A variation involves constructing a likeness of yourself to take your place while you escape. The basic premise is to have the authorities believe you are still in custody, thus affording you time to make good your escape.

- **The Trojan Horse:** As the name implies, it means hiding inside something else that would normally leave the prison without arousing suspicion. Successful escapes have been made hiding in body bags, coffins, laundry bags, garbage containers, and secret compartments built into various forms of transportation.

- **The Tunnel:** The last resort of escape strategies is *the tunnel.* Tunneling involves serious logistical problems: you would need digging tools, a facade to hide the opening of the tunnel, a way of dispensing of tons of dirt, wood planking to use in shoring the side and roof against cave-ins, a lighting system, and, depending on the length of the tunnel, a way to circulate fresh air to prevent suffocating.

Because of the logistical requirements and intensive labor, tunneling is usually a team project, yet despite the efforts required, tunneling has been used in many successful and dramatic escapes.

Escape Equipment

- ***Money:*** Have people from the outside supply you with the currency used in the system. Most successful escapes required bribing a guard to look the other way at the right time. Money is also needed to buy supplies from the prison black market and to buy protection. Without money, your chances of escape are drastically reduced. This is why Special Forces operatives, working behind enemy lines, are equipped with gold coins sewn into the lining of their equipment.

- ***Keys:*** Most escapes require getting through locked doors. Even a trained locksmith would have a difficult time picking the locks you would find in a security lock-up. The best method is to steal the key you need, make a copy, and then replace the original, since missing keys will alert authorities to an escape attempt and they will change the locks making the stolen key useless. Another method is to make an impression of the key in modeling clay, caulking compound, a bar of soft soap, or wax. The impression, or life-sized tracing, can then be smuggled out to cohorts to be copied, or, if you are good with your hands, you may be able to carve a copy from plastic, hardwood, or bone.

- **Identity Papers:** When on the run, you will eventually be required to provide identification papers. These can sometimes be obtained from fellow prisoners or bought or stolen from guards. If you have escaped without papers, the easiest way to obtain them is to go to a crowded area, wait until you find someone who most closely matches your description, and follow him until you have a chance to deprive him of his identification.

- **Maps and Compass:** An escape plan requires knowing where to go and how to get there which means you need a map. These can be smuggled or, as a last resort, drawn up from descriptions provided by fellow prisoners or jail staff. If your escape plan involves going cross-country, you will need a compass as well. If you cannot buy one, the old Boy Scout trick of using a magnetized needle inserted through a piece of cork or Styrofoam floated on a still pool of water may suffice.

- **Provisions:** Caloric requirements increase dramatically when you are on the run. Lack of adequate food and water will make you weak, slow you down, and reduce your mental sharpness, making you prone to injuries and mistakes that will get you recaptured.

If possible, buy extra provisions and stockpile the high calorie, non-perishables like biscuits, chocolate, and dried meat.

If extra food cannot be bought through the black market, then you will have to save some of your daily rations. Reduce your intake until enough has been stockpiled then eat the full rations again for a few days before the escape date to build up your body's reserves.

HAND SIGNALS

10 HERBS **THAT HEAL**

COUGHING? **ADD ROSEMARY**

The eucalyptol in this aromatic herb is study proven to loosen chest congestion, making phlegm easier to expel. Plus, rosemary is rich in anti-inflammatory tannins, which soothe a sore throat.

GOES WELL WITH

WHITE BEANS   POTATOES   POLENTA   APPLES

CRAMPY TUMMY? **ADD MINT**

Peppermint contains menthol, a natural plant compound that relaxes pain-inducing intestinal spasms.

This reduces belly discomfort by 40 percent.

GOES WELL WITH

EGGPLANT   TOMATOES   MELON   GREEN PEAS

MENSTRUAL CRAMPS? **ADD OREGANO**

Enjoying 2 tsp of fresh oregano daily during menstruation reduces or eliminates cramps. That's because this herb's thymol and carvacrol, relax uterine muscles to prevent painful contractions.

GOES WELL WITH

MUSHROOMS   TOMATOES   OLIVES   SQUASH

ACHY JOINTS? **ADD CURRY POWDER**

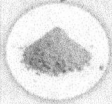

The curcumin in curry inhibits the body's production of prostaglandin E2, an inflammatory compound that over-sensitizes nerves. This blunts joing and muscle pain as effectively as prescirption medications.

GOES WELL WITH

LENTILS   RICE   CAULIFLOWER   SPINACH

UPSET GI TRACT? **ADD DILL**

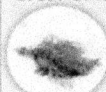

Indian scientists found that dill's limonene works as well as prescription antibiotics at killing harmful intestinal bacteria such as E. coli.

GOES WELL WITH

CUCUMBERS   BEETS   CARROTS   GREENS

BLOATED? **ADD PARSLEY**

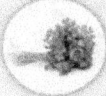

Thanks to its stores of apiol and myristicin, parsley is a natural diuretic that relieves bloat-inducing water retention by preventing salt from being reabsorbed into bodily tissue.

GOES WELL WITH

PASTA   TOMATOES   GRAINS   ONIONS

CONGESTED? **ADD CAYENNE**

The fiery capsaicin in cayenne deactivates substance P, a neurotransmitter linked to inflammation. The result is less sinus congestion and pressure.

GOES WELL WITH

LEAFY GREENS   BEANS   SOUPS   RICE

FEELING DOWN? **ADD BASIL**

The eugenol and rosmarinic acid in basil boost the brain's production of dopamine and serotonin. According to Indian researches, this could lead to sunnier moods in as little as three days.

GOES WELL WITH

TOMATOES   PIZZA   PASTA   OLIVES

FEELING TIRED? **ADD CILANTRO**

The carboxylic acid in cilantro binds to heavy metals such as mercury in the blood and carries them out of the body. Their removal reverses the toxin buildup that causes chronic fatigue, joint pain and depression.

GOES WELL WITH

AVOCADOS   CORN   BLACK BEANS   CURRIES

HAVING NAUSEA? **ADD GINGER**

Ginger's gingerol and shogaol calm digestive tract spasms to reduce nausea better than motion-sickness drugs.

GOES WELL WITH

POTATOES   MISO SOUP   RICE   PEARS

Character	Morse Code	Word
A	• —	Alfa
B	— • • •	Bravo
C	— • — •	Charlie
D	— • •	Delta
E	•	Echo
F	• • — •	Foxtrot
G	— — •	Golf
H	• • • •	Hotel
I	• •	India
J	• — — —	Juliett
K	— • —	Kilo
L	• — • •	Lima
M	— —	Mike
N	— •	November
O	— — —	Oscar
P	• — — •	Papa
Q	— — • —	Quebec
R	• — •	Romeo
S	• • •	Sierra
T	—	Tango
U	• • —	Uniform
V	• • • —	Victor
W	• — —	Whiskey
X	— • • —	Xray
Y	— • — —	Yankee
Z	— — • •	Zulu
1	• — — — —	One
2	• • — — —	Two
3	• • • — —	Three
4	• • • • —	Four
5	• • • • •	Five
6	— • • • •	Six
7	— — • • •	Seven
8	— — — • •	Eight
9	— — — — •	Nine
0	— — — — —	Zero

ABOUT THE AUTHOR

Balogun is Master Instructor and Technical Director of the *Afrikan Martial Arts Institute*, Co-Chair of the *Urban Survival Preparedness Institute* and Co-Chair / Founder of the *State of Black Science Fiction Convention*, the largest gathering of Black science fiction and fantasy creators and fans in the world.

He is the author of the bestselling non-fiction books: *Afrikan Martial Arts: Discovering the Warrior Within*, *The Afrikan Warriors' Bible*, *The Afrikan Warriors' Guide to Defeating Bullies and Trolls* and *Surviving the Urban Apocalypse* and ten novels, including, *MOSES: The Chronicles of Harriet Tubman (Books 1 & 2)* and *The Chronicles of Harriet Tubman: Freedonia*; *Redeemer*; *Once Upon A Time In Afrika*; *Fist of Africa*; *A Single Link* and *Wrath of the Siafu*; *The Scythe*; *The Keys*; and *Beneath the Shining Jewel*. Balogun is also contributing co-editor of three anthologies: *Ki: Khanga: The Anthology*, *Steamfunk* and *Dieselfunk* and contributing editor of the *Rococoa* anthology

Finally, Balogun is the Director and Fight Choreographer of the feature film, *Rite of Passage*, and the short films, *A Single Link*, *Rite of Passage: Initiation* and *The Dentist of Westminster* and co-author of the award winning screenplay, *Ngolo*.

www.ingramcontent.com/pod-product-compliance
Lightning Source LLC
Chambersburg PA
CBHW060233290526
45789CB00001B/34